JULIET REVELL

FROM
HELL TO GLORY
A WOMAN CALLED THEODOSIA

Kravitz & Sons
INNOVATORS IN PUBLISHING, MARKETING AND ADVERTISING

Kravitz and Sons LLC
204 E Arlington Blvd. Suite B
Greenville, NC 27858

Published by Kravitz and Sons LLC.

ISBN: 979-8-89639-380-1 (sc)
ISBN: 979-8-89639-379-5 (e)

TABLE OF CONTENTS

This book is dedicated to my mother Theodosia. Ever since that day when you asked me to write your story, a sense of joy began to emerge. The world will finally hear your story. From out of the darkness of physical abuse and pain you have become as a mighty prayer warrior and teacher of the bible. Your powerful story was meant to encourage someone who feels there is no way out. Numerous times you have stated, "To every person who is going through abuse, I want you to know that God knows what you are going through. He is the answer. He delivered me and he will deliver you. Call out to him and trust him."

We are the better because you took the back seat and pushed us forward. The seeds that you have sown in us are producing fruit in us. You taught us how to persevere through the difficult times by your courage to fight and not accept defeat. You taught us how to love by way you loved us and everyone that came across your path. You demonstrated the love of Christ through your daily walk with him. In the midst of your pain you taught us love conquers all. On behalf of all your children, Kevin, Kenneth, Angela, James Jr, Juliet, Jennifer, Milton and Adam in heaven, we say thank you for being such an amazing mother and we love you. This is your story.

FOREWORD

When my sister Juliet Revell asked me to write the foreword to this book you're holding in your hand, "From Hell To Glory" A Woman Called Theodosia" a quote attributed to Irenaeus, a theologian from the early Christian Church came to mind. *"The glory of life is to love, not to be loved; to give, not to get, to serve, not to be served, to be a cup of strength to any soul in a crisis of weakness."*

I cannot think of anyone who more exemplified, personified and actualized the above quotation than my mom Theodosia (July 23, 1936- September 30, 2024) "From Hell to Glory" is a book, but yet more than book. It is a tumultuous, strenuous journey of the heart-break of domestic abuse and how she shepherded and delivered us, her children out of a catastrophic environment to a place of safety.

In short, Mom was our Moses leading my siblings and myself (seven of us) through the red seas of life. But she did more than to get us to the promise land of safety, she modeled for us and grafted in the fabric of our being a legacy of faith in an unfailing Savior who make us "more than conquerors" through Christ who loved us and gave His life for us. We look forward to seeing you in heaven. We are following in your footsteps. We miss you deeply and love you dearly.

- Ken Revell

CHAPTER 1

The Courtship

I often wondered what things would be like in the Big Apple. Numerous thoughts ran through my mind. I am only fourteen years old, but for some reason, my life seems to be racing into adulthood. Living in Florida with my mother has made me very accustomed to the daily routine of household chores and unstated responsibilities ushered in through birth. Normally, chores often include cleaning, washing and ironing clothes, and cooking food. Two to three times a week, I would have to share chores at my grandmother's farm. The cows and hogs had to be fed. I had the distinct displeasure of milking the cows and chasing the chickens. The overpowering smell of farm animals would sometimes overtake my ability to keep from regurgitating my last meal. Leaving the animal kingdom has got to be a bonus sent from heaven. I must admit that I will miss the fun I had playing with my cousins and my two aunts, Thelma and Dot (short for Dorothy).

As an only child, I would get lonely at home with Mother, but when Thelma, Dot, and I were together, we had some of the best times. I wish they could come with me. Going to the farm wasn't all bad. I always felt that Grandma Florence treated me a little more special than the other grandchildren, even though I knew that she had no favorites. I guess the fact that Grandma Florence withheld spankings from me is enough for me to feel that I received a special favor.

There are so many things that will change when I go to New York. Thelma and Dot will be too far away for me to talk or play with. Why do I really have to go anyway? Daddy and Mother said that this move would provide a better environment and education for me, but why do I have to move all the way to New York? How is Mother going to make it here alone by herself? Who will help her cook and clean if I am not here? What if I do not like this school and no one wants to become my friend? I was confused and upset about all of this. First, Mother and Daddy got a divorce, and now I have to move to New York. I love both Mother and Daddy, but what did I do to make them not love me anymore?

Since I was having such a hard time trying to understand that divorce was not the result of something that I did, Mother and Daddy, both called me into the living room and said, "Theodosia, we want to talk to you." They both tried to explain that sometimes adults cannot continue to live together, but nothing will stop them from loving me. Daddy went on to explain that he went to New York to find a better job so that he could provide for me. While he was in New York, he got married again and now I have a stepmother who would love me just as much. They both reassured me that I could call Mother and come back to Florida for the summer months to spend time with her, Thelma, and Dot.

After I took some time to exhale, I gave some consideration to what Daddy and Mother said to me. It took me a while to accept, but what they said started to make sense. I started to think about some of the exciting things that Daddy said I could do in New York. Some of the places that he talked about sounded almost too good to be true. How else was I going to know if I did not go?

As the days drew closer to departure, I felt a growing anticipation building inside of me. Moreover, I can come back to spend the entire summer here in Florida and see Thelma and Dot and I can make up some of the lost time from the school year. Maybe moving to New York isn't as bad as I first thought.

Time for departure was approaching rapidly. My stepmother's phone call reaffirmed Daddy's promise that Mother, Daddy, and my stepmother would love me without fail. She was very kind and encouraging. Nevertheless, a sudden sadness and sense of joy came over me. Saying good-bye to Mother was something that I never thought would happen so soon. I hated saying good-bye to Thelma and Dot. It was also difficult saying good-bye to all our neighbors and friends. Nothing could stop the flow of tears as Mother, and I pulled up to the train station. We talked briefly and embraced each other before I got onto the train. Mother tried to reassure me that things would be better for me in New York, and she would be looking forward to seeing me during summer vacation. I boarded the train and looked out the window at Mother as the train departed.

There is no turning back now, I thought to myself. Shortly after departure, I saw a couple of girls on the train who went to school with me. They were going to see their parents who lived in New York for the summer. This was a normal, routine summer trip for them. The girls were very helpful to me on the train. They explained everything that I needed to know such as how the train would enter Penn Station. The girls and I remained together the entire train ride. I really enjoyed the train ride much better than I expected. We arrived at Penn Station exactly the way the girls explained it. I saw Daddy, and we embraced each other. "Wow, New York is nothing like Florida," I said out loud. I was amazed at all the tall buildings as Daddy drove us to his place.

My Arrival into New York

We arrived at Daddy's house in Inwood, New York. My stepmother greeted me with a very warm embrace and welcoming spirit. She had the table prepared and told me, "Help yourself Theodosia and make yourself at home." I was still amazed at all that I had seen so far. My eyes continued to roam throughout the house. This place was beautiful and was nothing like our house in Florida. After Daddy and Mother got divorced, Mother rented a small house. We did not have any of these luxuries that my eyes were appreciating. Immediately, my eyes became fixed on the television. We did not have one of those in Florida. My stepmother was watching the Dodgers baseball game. I found out later that she loved baseball. I continued to walk through the house in amazement. There was an indoor bathroom with a real tub and toilet. In Florida, we had an outhouse, and we took baths in a tin tub. This was great to see. I was getting excited. Next, Stepmother showed me to my room. It had a closet in the room. In Florida, we used a rod to hang everyone's clothes on. The room had a dresser with a mirror on it and a tall dresser for my clothes. I have never seen anything like this. I was almost speechless, to say the least.

From the outside of the house, I noticed that houses were attached to other houses. Wow, the neighbors were so physically close. We had some neighbors who lived upstairs in the same building. Many of the neighbors were very friendly and went out of the way to welcome me.

It took me a couple of days to get settled into a new environment. As time went on, I began to develop a dislike for my stepmother. She ran a very strict household. For example, she had certain foods that were hands off and other foods that I could eat or drink. I was okay with this because some food was put aside for her to prepare dinner. One of my first mistakes with her was drinking a glass of milk. Oh boy, she was mad at me. I thought that I could easily go to the store and buy another one. The thought never came to my mind that I would be causing a problem. I was thirsty, so I had a glass of milk. Sometimes my stepmother would babysit her two grandchildren. Since the children were toddlers, she got upset when I drank some of the milk set aside for them. Unfortunately, this is not the way my stepmother does things. Another mistake was when I tried to wash dishes but was told to sit down and enjoy myself. While living with Mother, I had more freedom because of the enormous responsibilities attached to that freedom.

I wasn't used to someone doing all the cooking and cleaning in the house and running the house like Stepmother did. This was unfamiliar territory for me. I wasn't sure how to not feel responsible for the daily upkeep of day-to-day chores. Stepmother explained to me that I should not worry about doing everything in the house. She stated that I should focus more on my homework and not be so concerned about the major household affairs. My stepmother also told me that everyone else calls her Mom, so she would like it if I called her mom also. From that point on, I called her Mom, and I continued to call my natural mom Mother. Listening to Mom made sense because I had failed to realize that I was missing out on my teenage years.

I did not understand much until later I realized Mom truly cared and only wanted the best for me. Mom kept a very clean house, and she expected everyone to keep it that way. I always felt that her eyesight was beyond 20/20. She could see a drop of water or food crumbs so small that the average person would need a magnifying glass to see it. I believe that Mom would see it from any room in the house.

Mom refused to use a mop to clean the floor. She would get down on her knees and use a rag and a scrub brush to clean floors. She would also wax the floors in the same manner. After Mom finished the floors, she would wash the rags and brushes with bleach for reuse. Mom taught me to make sure that when I go out, I am dressed neatly, and my clothes are ironed and without wrinkles. Sometimes Mom's obsession with cleanliness and perfection made it hard for me to totally embrace her efforts to demonstrate her love toward me. At times, I would get fed up, and Daddy would come to my rescue. I learned to just accept her ways and follow her instructions. Despite all the strict rules employed by my Mom, I was able to learn and enjoy wonderful Bible studies in our home and entertain family and friends on special occasions. I also developed wonderful friendships that I cherish to this day.

One of our neighbors, Nancy, became my first friend. She welcomed me and introduced me to Edith, Catherine, and Doris. All of us hung out together and lived in the same neighborhood. We walked to school together and experienced some wonderful times laughing and playing.

My first day at Lawrence High School in New York was in September 1950. I was scared and nervous because I did not know the teachers or the students. To my surprise, the teachers and the students made me feel more comfortable. They wanted to know about Florida, which was exciting to them. They did not realize that learning about New York was exciting to me. My school day became a normal routine day. I enjoyed playing on the volleyball team. We would practice after school and have games on Saturday.

Shortly afterward, I got a babysitting job for a Jewish family. Monday through Friday I would go straight to their house after school to babysit. I would not go back home until the weekend. Someone found out that I was catching the bus coming from another county to school. The police showed up at my daddy's home and asked why I was coming from another county to attend Lawrence High School. As a result, I had to give up this job.

After two years, we moved from Inwood, New York located in Nassau County to Jamaica in Queens County. Daddy found a three-bedroom apartment, which was a better and larger place for us to live. Daddy gave me three schools to choose from. I chose Jamaica High because it seemed the better of the three schools. I made the transition to Jamaica but really missed my friends in Inwood. I met new friends from the neighborhood who were very friendly. My friends and I went to Jamaica High together using public transportation. Jamaica High was approximately two miles from home. During my senior year at Jamaica High, I went to school from 7:00 a.m. to 12:00 p.m. I found another babysitting job, which was right across the street from Jamaica High. Some of my responsibilities in babysitting included taking the baby to the park and running errands. I worked from 12:30 p.m. to 6:30 p.m. and then caught the bus back home. I was able to use my bus pass for a month, which was convenient for me because as a student I could use the same bus pass until 7:00 p.m.

New York had a curfew; no one under the age of eighteen was allowed on the streets after 10:00 p.m. If caught on the streets, the police would take the child to their parents, and the parents would be questioned why their child was out past the curfew. I remember the night of my junior prom in which my date and I were caught by the police about to catch a cab home. The police asked us, "Where are you going?" We told him we were coming from the prom and about to take a cab home. The police told us to go straight home, and he better not see us again.

My friends and I enjoyed spending time together on the weekends. We were all very close friends and looked out for each other. Since we lived in the same neighborhood, it was easy for us to leave together to go hang out. I will always remember the twin brothers Levon and Leon, whom we called Bonnie and Pig, and the girls Sonya and Genevieve.

Bonnie and Pig were more like brothers to me. Our houses were so close that I could look out of our window and see into their house. Sometimes we went to the movies, the ice cream parlor, and the skating rink to have some fun. Our time together was filled with laughter, fun, and many memorable moments.

A moment that marked a significant change during my life was on a Sunday afternoon after church. My friends and I decided to go to the ice cream parlor on Merritt Boulevard, approximately three to four blocks from home. I approached the counter to ask for a strawberry ice cream soda when a young man about my age asked to pay for my ice cream soda. Initially, I refused his offer, but he was very persistent.

Eventually, I gave in and allowed him to pay for my ice cream soda. I turned around and saw my friends Bonnie and Pigg, who came to the stool where I was sitting. To my surprise, the twins knew who this young man was and introduced him to me as James. I was shocked when they told me that James was their first cousin.

After finishing my ice cream soda, I got ready to leave, and James asked me where I was going. I told him that I was going back to church to attend the 3:00 p.m. service. He asked me if he could go with me. I replied with a very firm no. I proceeded to go to church, and I had no idea where James went. The next day, Monday, the twin brothers and one of my friends (who had a crush on me) came to my house. As friends, it was not unusual for us to visit each other's house, but this time James came with them. While at my house, all five of us made plans to go skating together on Saturday. My friend who had a crush on me was supposed to be my date that night. When Saturday night came around and it was time to go skating, only one person showed up: James. Hmm. That seemed quite odd, but I did not argue. I went along for the ride.

We arrived at the skating rink and found out quickly that James was a natural skater, and I mastered the art of holding onto the floor. James tried so hard to teach me how to skate, but my two feet refused to listen to my brain or to James. I fell at the skating rink so many times that I could not go to church the next Sunday. James came by and asked Mom if he could see me. Mom told him no because I was still in bed. I was too embarrassed to show all my bruises from the skating rink.

The next weekend, James sent a beautiful card in the mail expressing how much he cared for me and asked me if I would go steady with him. The words were so beautifully written that I accepted his request. We started dating from that point on. James brought me gifts such as beautiful earrings, scarves, and chocolates. Every weekend we went on dates to the movies and danced at the teenage clubs.

James displayed considerable kindness on our dates. He paid for our bus fares, movie tickets, and everything else. We had a wonderful time getting to know each other and enjoying each moment together. I can still remember some of the movies that we saw, such as *Lady and the Tramp* and a popular song "Que Sera Sera" from the movie we saw, *The Man Who Knew Too Much*. There was an interesting parallel between the movie *Lady and the Tramp* and my life.

I enjoyed the movies and how James's gentleman qualities came on display. Some of the other places that we went on dates included Central Park and the Apollo Theatre in Harlem to see entertainment. James was consistent in displaying gentleman qualities as we walked down the streets together after all my chores were done. James began to express his love for me and would tell me that he wanted to marry me. He promised that he would never hit me. He stated that he wanted children but not many. James was working with his uncle Herman at that time. The twin brothers were James's Uncle Herman's children. This is how James and the twin brothers were first cousins. We continued to go dancing and date each weekend. I truly enjoyed every moment.

One Saturday, my friends and I decided to go to the beach without James. James came to the house and asked Daddy who I went with to the beach. Daddy told James three guys and one girl. James got very upset. James came back that evening and asked why we did not come by to pick him up. I told him that they did not ask him to go to the beach and that we were not married. James got extremely angry and told me to never play that trick on him again. He also went on to say, "If I don't go, you don't go!"

James did not come around for a few days. The statement he made really bothered me. I hesitated, thinking that I did not want to go out with him again. A couple of days later, James came by with gifts and apologized for what he said to me. I accepted his apology because I felt he deserved a second chance. On the other hand, my mom said that she saw something in him that was not right. It was her strong opinion that I should not marry James. He was not the right person for me. Daddy and I talked, and we did not agree with Mom. Daddy felt like James was a very nice guy. The next weekend, we went dancing. While walking home, James told me that he was in love with me and wanted to spend the rest of his life with me. He asked me to marry him. I replied, "Yes." Two weeks later, he brought a ring from the five-and-ten-cents store and officially proposed to me. I was excited and told Daddy, and he was excited. Mom said that she still does not feel right about him. I never questioned Mom about why she felt that way.

CHAPTER 2

My New Life

Who would have ever imagined five years ago that I would be making wedding plans? I was so afraid of leaving the only life that I knew in Florida, and now at the age of nineteen, my life is once again emerging into something new. While James and I continued to spend more time together, my heart fell deeper in love. Our time together resembled the making of a beautiful poem. Line by line, the story unveils. James continued to display his desire to spend time with me in the most unexpected ways. He would come over to our house and help me with my chores. I was pleasantly surprised to see James vacuum and clean our bathrooms. He was a very clean person who went out of his way to help me in any way possible. Mom was so impressed by his willingness to come over and clean that one time Mom's tone sounded a bit envious when she said, "I can never get your dad to help me clean." This went on every weekend until we were married.

Numerous plans had to be made for our wedding day. James and I did not know where to begin in planning such a special occasion. I talked it over with Daddy and Mom, and they both agreed that it would be better to have the wedding at our house. This would save an enormous amount of money. Neither one of us had any money to pay for a wedding.

I had already graduated from high school; James was working with his Uncle Herman in Jamaica. James decided he would not return to school after the eleventh grade. He lived with his uncle Fred and aunt Flo (Florence) upstairs in Jamaica before moving with them to St. Albans. James had a unique relationship with his family at this time. Part of his family, one sister and one brother, purchased a house together in St. Albans. The house was designed like a duplex, with two apartments separated by a flight of stairs inside, which made access much easier between the two apartments. Upstairs was occupied by James's uncle Fred and aunt Flo and downstairs was occupied by his uncle Herman and aunt Lucille. James's uncle Herman was actually his uncle-in-law because he was married to his aunt Lucille. Everyone got along really well considering the amount of people residing in the house.

When James's family received the news that we were engaged to get married, everyone got excited. I had frequently visited James's family in St. Albans with my friends the twins, Leon and Levon, who lived practically next door. On the weekends, we would hang out together, and I would go with them to their father's house. James's uncle Herman is the twins' father. His uncle Herman and aunt Lucille and uncle Fred and Aunt Flo all welcomed me and made me feel like family each time I came over. I did not know James when the twins and I used to go to Herman's house.

I was introduced to James's parents via telephone. Both parents welcomed me into the family, and they gave us their blessings. His mother was very nice to me and said to James, "I hope that you will be good to my daughter." I never got a chance to meet her in person. James's father and mother really liked me. James's father would tease James often by telling him that I was his wife. James's mother advised him, "Take good care of your wife, and do not to mistreat her." I also had the opportunity to meet James's grandmother Carrie. This was his father's mother. Grandmother Carrie lived with Aunt Flo and Uncle Fred and James. Uncle Fred was a very funny man who loved to dance. I liked Uncle Fred also because he stood up for me. I did not get to meet the rest of James's family at this time. However, I wanted James to meet my mother.

Since Mother was in Florida, we called her on the telephone to share the news of our engagement. Mother had remarried Albert

Carter, who was called Papa Albert for short. We spoke to both of them. They were very happy for us and welcomed James as his son-in-law. We were grateful to receive their blessings for our new life. I discussed with Mother the plans to have our wedding at Daddy's house. I explained to her how having it there would save us a lot of money. I wanted deeply for Mother to come to one of the most special days of my life. Mother expressed how deeply she wanted to be there for me. However, she went on to explain that it would be better for her to come after we have moved into a place of our own. She did not feel very comfortable coming to Daddy's home since they were divorced. She was also left with the question of where she would reside while in New York. Everything she said made sense to me. While I was a bit saddened, I understood fully.

Wedding Plans

I know that it had been almost a year, but it felt like yesterday when James proposed to me. As our wedding day drew near, I realized that I did not know the first thing about planning a wedding. I was so glad that Mom volunteered to help plan my wedding. There were so many decisions I had to make. I needed to find the most beautiful dress in the world and the perfect shoes and accessories to match. I was so excited that it was hard for me to keep focused. It was really great that I had so much help now. My family had been so wonderful to me. Mom spoke to Uncle Thomas, Daddy's brother, and his wife, Aunt Estelle, to help. Before long, we ended up having Mom, Aunt Estelle, Mrs. Bell, and Mrs. Hacker making all the food arrangements for our big day. Each of these wonderful ladies was amazing cooks, who turned cooking into a work of art and a taste that left us craving for more. Mr. and Mrs. Hacker had become very close friends of Daddy and Mom. We went to the same church in Far Rockaway. The Hackers were like family that we could always count on. Mr. Hacker agreed to make my wedding cake, another tremendous blessing that saved us money and time.

Since the food arrangements were coming together so nicely, I needed to start looking for a dress. Daddy, Mom, and I went to Jamaica Avenue to look for a dress. We visited three bridal shops in search of the perfect dress. As we walked through the different shops, Mom and

I were more in tune with the touch and feel of the various fabrics. On the other hand, Daddy began to grow tiresome. At last, we arrived at the third bridal shop, and we found a very beautiful baby-blue dress. This ankle-length dress was made of chiffon and lace stitched with a bateau neckline that follows the curve of the collarbone to the tip of the shoulders. The waistline hits the natural waist, providing a slenderizing effect at the waist. This exquisite dress was made from a delicate, sheer, and transparent chiffon material. The chiffon material added an extra touch of elegance, which flared perfectly from the waistline to the ankles to produce a stunning effect on me. The short sleeves added the perfect covering for the arms for this time of the year. I did not have money to pay for a traditional style wedding gown with a long train. I was very satisfied with our findings. The dress was not only my favorite color, but the fit was also exquisite. I knew without a doubt I would take James's breath away in this dress.

We went to a couple of shoe stores and were able to find the same shade of blue shoes to accentuate my dress. It's an unbelievably perfect match for my dress. We continued shopping and found beautiful accessories for me to wear.

Instead of wearing a veil, I decided to look for beautiful hair accessories to place in my hair. In one of the stores, we found a gorgeous hairpiece that was made as a small comb with baby-blue flowers and white pearls interconnected. I had to have this exquisite hairpiece. I also found the most beautiful pair of see-through white lace mitts that are worn from the elbow extending to the wrist, leaving the hands exposed. This will add an extra touch of elegance needed to make me feel glamorous. Daddy was becoming a little impatient, but as agreed, he paid for my dress, and I was well on my way to becoming a bride.

The wedding day arrived, and the excitement was increasing each moment. I caught a bus to Jamaica Avenue in hopes that James would not see me before the wedding. I made it back without running into him. I did not want him to see me until it was time for our wedding vows. Meanwhile at the house, the ladies worked hard in preparing a wonderful full course meal for everyone to enjoy immediately after we had declared our vows. The ladies had decorated the house with a variety of pastel-colored flowers throughout. The dining room table was laced with a beautiful tablecloth and elegant napkins set for the reception. A stand from the florist was placed at the entrance way of the living room for us to stand under to give our vows. The decor was full of soft-petal flowers, white lace, and the smell of love created an atmosphere perfect for wedding vows.

It was a late Saturday evening in January. The weather was pleasant and not too cold for this time of the year. Our guests had arrived with smiles and warm embraces for the two of us. Approximately thirty people were in attendance on this day. Most were family and some friends. Reverend Lewter was the presiding minister for our ceremony. Because I was a bit nervous, I asked Reverend Lewter if it was okay for us to face him and not our guest. I realized this meant our backs would be facing our guests, but I was afraid that if I had to face our guests during our vows, I would become more nervous.

Time had arrived for us to give our vows. I stood near James in the most beautiful baby-blue dress and matching baby-blue shoes. My hair was perfectly styled up with the placement of my gorgeous hair accessories. The soft white pearls and the baby blue flowers glimmered with the style of my dress. As Reverend Lewter was about to begin the ceremony, my eyes captured a glimpse of James's knees shaking severely. I know that I was a bit nervous, but James's knees looked a bit out of control. I wonder if I was the only one who noticed his knees. Reverend Lewter continued with the ceremony, and the both of us said our vows to one another. I was delighted to have one of my dearest friends, Bernice, as my maid of honor. One of the twins stood next to James as his best man. We made it through the ceremony without any problems even though we both were very nervous. After the ceremony, we embraced Mom and Daddy and all our family and friends in attendance.

Everyone congratulated us and wished us well for our new life. *Wow, I'm married!* It will take a moment for that to sink in.

Everyone's attention flowed into the extended dining room area for our reception. The display of food was inviting. The ladies prepared a mix of ham, fried chicken, potato salad, macaroni and cheese, and a few different green vegetables. For dessert, we had the cutting of our wedding cake and fresh fruits. All our guests enjoyed the food. One of my cousins ate so much food, and he stuffed his pockets with food. Our reception turned out to be a wonderful family-and-friends gathering. For approximately two hours, my family and friends made this day a very special day to remember. My only sadness was the absence of Mother.

As the day ended and our guests began to depart, Gwendolyn asked if we would take her home to Inwood. Gwendolyn was Daddy's brother, my Uncle Thomas's daughter. We agreed to take her home, so the five of us—James, his cousin, Nancy, Gwendolyn, and I— all jumped in the car for a nice stroll. James's cousin and Nancy sat in the front seat while Gwendolyn sat in the back seat with James and me. We had a nice time riding in the back seat like celebrities. We laughed and talked about several things until we heard and felt the pressure deflated in one of our tires. We pulled over and got out of the car while James changed the flat tire. James was naturally gifted with using his hands, so changing a tire was not a challenge for him. We got back in the car and back on the road. We arrived safely at Gwendolyn's house and said good night to her. We made it back to my parents' house without any additional problems.

We could not afford a honeymoon, so our night ended together at their house. James and I had applied for an apartment for the two of us, but it wasn't going to be ready for at least two weeks. My room was too small for the two of us to use, so we camped out in my parents' living room. We were grateful for all the hospitality provided by my parents. The living room sofa extended into a bed, providing us with a makeshift bedroom. We were content with the arrangements because we knew our place would be ready in only a couple of weeks.

Wow! This is my wedding night, and I am a newlywed. This will take some time for me to get used to this. My feelings were somewhat mixed between the excitement of our marriage and thoughts of becoming the perfect wife. I realized that there were responsibilities that came along with my new role in life. James and I talked about several things on our wedding night. We talked about a honeymoon, but at that point, we did not know how we could bring our dreams into fruition. A trip to the Bahamas that James promised me would have placed the ice cream on top of our wedding dream. For that moment, that dream was on hold. We were both happy for the two of us that special night.

During this two-week period, James and I continued to enjoy our time together. We went to the movies, and we took long walks at night. We made the best of each moment that we had together. James was working at Kew Gardens Apartments in maintenance, and my job was cleaning houses (also called day's work). As the two-week mark rapidly approached, the landlord, a very nice West Indies man contacted James and told us about our new apartment in St. Albans was ready and gave us a move-in date. Both of us were excited. We went to a furniture store and bought a three-room package deal, which consisted of a living room group, a kitchen table and chairs, and a complete white bedroom set, all for five hundred dollars. Dad and Mom agreed to help us make the payments for our furniture. We decided to leave the furniture at the store until our move-in date, and the furniture store agreed to deliver the furniture to our new apartment.

Our First Apartment

Our new apartment is a large one-bedroom apartment located upstairs of a two- story house. The house was built with the design of two separate apartments. For entrance into our apartment, we would use the private entrance door around the side of the house patio. The door to our apartment opens directly into our kitchen. The kitchen is a very important aspect of any dwelling place for a woman. The white-painted walls throughout the apartment illuminated a spacious and clean and wholesome environment. The kitchen came equipped with a sink, stove, and refrigerator. Four large cabinets were situated directly above the sink area. I was not bothered by the lack of cabinets below the sink area. The sink and the refrigerator were located on one side and the stove on the other side. The kitchen floor was lined with linoleum flooring, which was inexpensive but easy to care for.

When exiting the kitchen, we would step down into the dining room area. In the dining room area, we positioned our China cabinet against the wall and centered our table and four chairs to bring about a semiformal room for eating. Decorative rugs were placed under the dining room table and throughout the apartment to infuse space with color, offering comfort to the feet and to reduce noise. Since the remainder of the apartment was accented with beautiful wooden flooring, the decorative rugs added the missing element.

The dining room area was adjoined to a hallway that led to the bedroom and the living room. Our bedroom had a fully adjoined bathroom, which provided ample privacy while in the room. The furniture for our white bedroom included a queen-size bed, a dresser and mirror, and a chest with drawers. The bathroom came equipped with a sink, a mirror and a tub, and toilet. To get to the living room area, we had to exit our bedroom and go through the hallway to enter the living room. Our living room furniture included a three-piece sofa bed, love seat, and chair and a coffee table and two end tables. The living room provided us with a warm and inviting place to entertain guests.

Now that we were in our own place, we could take our time making it our own. I took some time to hang pictures and curtains for privacy. Since this was our first apartment and we were beginning a new journey, I was pleased with the size and amenities of our new home.

Our landlord was wonderful. Every time something broke, he fixed it right away. Having a landlord living downstairs was an added benefit. We did not have to wait long to get things done. I really enjoyed the neighborhood. The neighbors were very friendly and offered to help when needed.

After we moved into our own place, I was very concerned about fulfilling my duties as a wife. I kept the apartment very clean, and I took care of the cooking. James and I were also working at this time. The first six months of living in our own place were very nice. We did not have any significant events that took place. Each day started to feel rather routine. James would help me when I needed help around the apartment. We both were happy that our move went smoothly, and we were able to support ourselves. The rent for our apartment was eighty dollars per month. With the two of us working and minimal overhead expenses, we felt that we started in a positive position.

Shortly after we moved in and were settled, Mom came over to our apartment on one of her regular visits. Mom continues to impose her extreme cleaning personality everywhere she goes. When Mom walks into family members' homes, she takes it upon herself to clean anything that is dirty, straighten everything that is out of place, and invite herself to everyone's personal belongings. This trait of Mom is frowned upon by every family member. Mom's daughter, Ella Mae, my stepsister, hates to see her come to her house because she knows that Mom can become quite difficult. We are all challenged in trying to please her when it comes to cleanliness, but anything short of perfection will only trigger a cleaning rampage by Mom. Regardless of Mom's attempt for cleaning perfection, she is genuine at heart and a loving person.

During this visit, Mom took matters upon herself to straighten the clothes in our drawers. Of course, she was not asked to do so, but I would not have been able to stop her. As she rambled through James's underclothes, she discovered bottles of alcohol hidden in the drawers. We both were shocked.

Mom yelled out to me, "Did you know your husband drinks?"

I replied, "No, that's very shocking."

"You don't go into his drawers to see what's in it?"

"Mom that thought never came across my mind. I cannot believe that I did not see this."

Mom and I talked about this at length. I started to wonder if this was why James's knees shook uncontrollably during our wedding. He appeared normal to me on our wedding day except for his knees. James was keeping his drinking from me all this time. I wondered when he started drinking. Why was he hiding alcohol in the drawers? These thoughts were running through my mind, but I was afraid to verbalize any of this with Mom. We agreed to confront him. Mom told Daddy beforehand, and the three of us talked to James at my parents' house.

Daddy started the conversation by telling James that he knew that he had been drinking. Daddy said, "I love you, and I do not hate you. You need help. Alcohol will not solve problems."

James replied, "I do not have a problem. I can stop drinking at any time."

Daddy responded, "You cannot stop drinking anytime you want to. You need help. You need to ask the Lord to help you." "I will try to do better."

Daddy tried hard to convince James that he had a problem and needed help, but to no avail. Daddy handled the situation extremely well, and the conversation ended peacefully. Daddy was gracious and not overbearing with James. However, James refused to acknowledge that he had a drinking problem or that he needed help. Mom pulled me aside privately in the kitchen and said,

"Keep your eyes open. He is subject to do anything when he gets angry."

I replied, "Okay, I will."

We took the city bus back home. James did not appear mad about us confronting him that night. I did not bring up the conversation with him on the bus or at home. I decided to give James time to absorb what Daddy said to him.

It was not long before James started to voice his desire to spend time with the boys.

I was not exactly sure what made James so anxious to get out with the boys, but I did not try to stop him. I did not know if he felt trapped by marriage or just needed to exhale for a moment. James started to frequent the bar on the corner of the street that we lived on. On the weekend, he would go to the bar for about an hour and then return home to check on me. Then after a short period, he would go back to the bar. According to James, he was going back to hang out with the boys. James would drink and would drink all day from Friday night through part of Sunday. He would try to sober up in time to go to work on Monday.

James's new passion for the bar continued for quite some time. He invited me to come a few times, but I declined. I did not drink alcohol, and I knew that I would not feel comfortable in a bar even if I was with James.

One night, James came from the bar drunk, and he accused me of seeing another man. He said that he saw a man coming out of our apartment. This person did not exist, but James would not listen to anything I said. In the midst of his drunken anger, he struck me with his hands across the face and physically hurt me. This was the first time that James had ever touched me in a harmful manner.

After he realized that he hit me, he apologized by saying he was sorry and that he would never hit me again. This behavior became a repeated trend with James. He would go to the bar, get drunk, come home, accuse me of other men that did not exist, and hit me again and again. I did not know what to do or think. Why was James treating me so badly? I would try to get him to see that he was not making any sense, but he would just become more abusive. I fought with everything in me to stop him, but James was like a raging bull when he was under the influence of alcohol.

I had come to realize that James was an extremely jealous person when it concerns me. I never gave him a reason to think that I was stepping outside of our wedding vows. I worked hard to make our marriage work, but James continued to abuse me physically, verbally, and emotionally.

I tried to hide the bruises and scars he inflicted on everyone, including my parents. I knew that as soon as someone saw the bruises on my body, trouble was sure to follow. I worried most about what Daddy would do to James if he ever found out. This thought scared me the most because I am Daddy's only child. I worked hard to make our marriage work. Mother and Daddy's divorce left an unpleasant effect on me. I never dreamed that my marriage would end this way. What was I to do? Who, if there are any, could I talk to? I was scared of what James may do if I told someone. His behavior is more irrational each day. I was so confused and scared of James. But maybe if I could hang in there a little longer, James would change.

A couple of weeks later, James was drinking again. Out of the blue, James yells out, "Your parents need to stay out of my business." I do not know what triggered him to say this. It had been two weeks since the conversation with my parents and I had not brought this up since that night. It was apparent to me that this must have been on his mind the past two weeks even though he had not said anything until now. I never knew what would come out of James's mouth.

About one month later, Daddy came over to drop something off for me, and James got upset. In anger, James yelled out, "He don't have to keep bringing you stuff. I have enough money to take care of you."

I told James, "You said that you don't have enough money to afford these things, so why do you have a problem with Daddy bringing these things to me?" James got angry and hit me again. I yelled at him, "Why did you hit me? You promised me that you will never hit me again!"

We argued until James had lain across the bed and went to sleep. The next day, we were still both angry, but we were tired of arguing. I told him, "If you want to argue, argue with yourself!" Nothing else happened that day. For nearly one month, things were tense between us but without incident.

On another occasion, two of our friends, a husband and wife, came over to our apartment. James spoke very nicely to the husband as if nothing was wrong. After their visit, James accused me of having a fling with this man. James said this man was my boyfriend, and he was coming to see me while he was at work. Every so often, James would bring up this accusation again.

On a different occasion a man was passing by the house and spoke to the both of us. James accused me of seeing this guy also while he was at work. I explained this to James that none of his accusations were true. He never believed me or accepted anything I said in my defense. These arguments were never ending. I was glad that on both of those occasions, James did not lay a hand on me.

We had been married a year, and James was still abusive both physically and verbally. At one point, I suspected that I may be pregnant, so I went to the doctor. The doctor confirmed my suspicions and told me I was about six weeks pregnant. I broke the news to James, and he was ecstatic over the thought of becoming a daddy. I could still remember conversations during our long walks in which James expressed his desire for children. I wondered if becoming a father would have any impact on the way James treated me.

Because of my pregnancy, a number of things would have to change for me. From that point, I would have to take extra care of myself since I was having another life growing inside of me. The doctor explained the importance of prenatal care and monthly doctor's appointments that I must not miss. I would catch the bus once a month to go to my doctor's appointments. Sometimes, if James got off work early, he would come with me to the doctor. Most of the time, I went to the doctor by myself.

James's behavior improved slightly. He did not drink as much, and he bragged about becoming a proud papa. But this good behavior was short-lived. James began to drink heavily again. One night, during one of James's drunken episodes, he became very angry and raised his hand to hit me.

When he raised his hand, I told him, "If you hit me, you will go to jail this night because I am pregnant!" He actually thought about what I said to him for once, and he withdrew his hand. For the remainder of that pregnancy, James did not raise his hand to hit me again. I was very surprised to see some of James's good qualities start to emerge. James actually began to pamper me with flowers, perfume, jewelry, and some of my favorite foods. He would wash dishes and was very thoughtful and helpful throughout the pregnancy. I enjoyed the pampering, even though deep down inside, I knew he was just guilty.

Time to Deliver

I went into labor one Saturday night and was rushed to the hospital. The labor was intense and long. I suffered for a long time because the baby was not in a hurry. I did not give birth on Saturday or Sunday, so the doctor told James that I would not deliver that night. "So go home and get some sleep and come back in the morning," the doctor advised him.

We did not have a phone, so there was no way to call James if something happened. Monday morning, before James came back to the hospital, the baby was finally ready to make a grand entrance into the world. Before giving birth, the doctor said, "This is going to be a big baby."

I gave birth to one child and was relieved that it was over and he was alive and healthy. About ten minutes later, the doctor said, "Here comes another one!" I was shocked and delivered a second son. When James finally arrived at the hospital, the doctor gave him the news that I had delivered two babies, a set of twins. James was so happy that he started calling people to share the news and bragging on being the father of twin boys. I called Mother and told Papa Albert. He immediately tried to wake Mother, but she was difficult to wake. When he told her later, she almost passed out. She yelled, "That's what I wanted!" Both of them were excited about the news.

After childbirth, I ran a fever, lost a lot of blood, and had to be treated for anemia. After seven days in the hospital, the twins and I were released to go home. Dad and Mom came to pick us up from the hospital. I was very blessed that the doctor ordered a nurse to help me and to help with the care of the twins for one month. The nurse remained at our apartment for the entire month. The nurse was very nice and taught me how to rotate feeding the twins and more so that I can also get some sleep and rest. I was very grateful for all the help that I received from the nurse and from Mom, who came over often to assist me and the twins. Mom would also cook food for us and bring it over to us. She was such a blessing when I needed her most. As for the twins' names, they were called A-Baby and B- Baby for about two to three weeks until we came up with the names Kevin and Kenneth. James helped me by getting up for the twins at night for about two months. That was as long as James lasted. After the second month, James would not wake up during the night and was almost useless.

Dad paid for diaper service delivery straight to our apartment for one year. This was truly a wonderful gift. The diaper service brought new diapers and picked up the dirty diapers each week. Cloth diapers were the only type of diapers that were available at that time. Cleaning diapers had been a challenging task to add to raising newborn twins.

A baby- product manufacturing company sent clothes for our twins for one year for free. This company also kept me supplied with baby products such as baby lotion, baby oil, Desitin, blankets, and so on. I was also given a one-month supply of Pet Milk, Karo Syrup (to mix with the baby formula), baby bottles, brushes to clean baby bottles, and more. The manufacturing company wanted to put me in their commercials to advertise their baby products, but James would not let me. This would have given us some good income.

After a couple of months, James's good behavior started to fizzle out. James wanted attention. He started to demand food to be ready when he came home, and he wanted me to spend a lot of time with him. James would not admit it, but he was jealous of the twins. He felt the twins were getting more of my attention and time. This was an extremely difficult time in my life, and James did not lighten the load. He made my load more burdensome. Taking care of newborns and trying to regain my health was already overwhelming. I was physically sick and emotionally drained, but I continued to push myself anyway. Because of my anemia problem, I had to go to the doctor twice a week to receive B-12 shots for treatment. I was stressed and lost a lot of weight to the point that I weighed less than 120 pounds.

James started going back to the bar more often this time, especially on the weekend. James was an added problem rather than a help to me. He started again with the arguments and accusing me with being involved with other men. There was no room for another man in my life, and James refused to acknowledge how much demand was placed on me between the twins and him. I felt like I resided at the bottom of the list of priorities in this household.

Jealously, anger, and the demand for attention, coupled with alcohol abuse, made James like a bomb on the verge of explosion. In his anger, jealousy, and drunken state of mind, James went as far as saying that he did not think the twins were his. Oftentimes, in an angry rage, James would punch holes in the walls, break furniture, and snatch towel racks out of the bathroom walls with his hands. There were many times that I could not figure out what triggered his rage of anger.

After the twins were a year old, I went back to work again. I found a babysitter who charged me five dollars a day from Monday through Friday. I worked cleaning two houses a day from 8:00 a.m. to 3:00 p.m. I made twenty dollars per day or one hundred dollars a week. I would get up early to take the twins to the babysitter. I picked up the twins at 4:00 p.m. from the sitter.

My babysitter's name was Mrs. George. She was a wonderful lady. She and her husband were extremely kind to me. One day, I came to pick up the twins, and Mrs. George knew that I had problems. She noticed the bruises on my face and body, and she questioned me. I tried to pretend as if I had fallen and hurt myself, but she was not accepting my lie. She said,

"I know that bruise you have on you. I have been through what you are going through. Your husband has been hitting you, right?"

"Yes, but I did not want to say anything."

"It's okay, you can talk to me. I have been through this type of situation before.

Honey, you do not have to put up with that. There are all kinds of help available. You can get help now. He can't touch you or hurt you."

I listened to her. It was kind of sinking in, and at the same time, it wasn't sinking in. She said, "You take care of your children. You be good to those children."

"Oh, I will."

"I have been through the same thing. My first husband beat me, so I left him." Mrs. George went on telling me what happened to her. She offered to help me with anything that I needed. Her husband was also very helpful to me. At that point, she would not charge me any money for babysitting. She told me, "Do not let James know that you are not taking any money from me. I am doing this to help you." She would give them a bath before I picked them up so that I would not have to bathe them when I got home. I was always grateful to Mrs. George. Her husband, Mr. George, was a World War II veteran hero. He was asked to give speeches on numerous occasions on veteran holidays. I will never forget these two wonderful people.

I worked for about a year until the twins were about two years old. One day, I was feeling very sick in my stomach to the point that I went to the doctor. The doctor told me that I had fibroid tumors and that I would not be able to have any more children. After leaving the doctor's office, I went home and prayed to God. I asked Him to remove whatever it was.

On the next day, Sunday, I went on a fast from 6:00 a.m. until 6:00 p.m. I had a scheduled doctor's appointment on Monday with a gynecologist. During my appointment at the clinic, three different doctors could not find anything. There was no sign of any tumors anywhere. I was convinced that God was with me and taking care of me. Later on, we were forced to move because of James's destructive behavior that he imposed on the house. The landlord came and said that we had to move. He gave us two weeks to leave. He spoke to me on a separate occasion.

"I'm not mad at you, but your husband is destroying my house and I'm tired of having to fix everything that he breaks." At that time, I had just found out that I was pregnant again, so I had to quit work. Fortunately, we were able to find another place within the two-week period that the landlord granted us. I was grateful to God for not allowing us to become homeless.

CHAPTER 3

Springfield Gardens

It was unfortunate that we had to move, but I was glad that we were able to find a place before our two weeks expired. Moving was more challenging for us this time because we have twins and I was pregnant again. Our new place was in Springfield Gardens; it was only about four to five miles from our St. Albans apartment. I did everything that I could to help pack, but my pregnancy limited my physical abilities. Daddy knew someone with a pickup truck to help us move, and James had his cousins to help us move.

The new apartment was like the St. Albans apartment. It was an upstairs apartment. This apartment was larger than St. Albans apartment. This was a two-bedroom, one-bathroom apartment with larger living space. The rent was $150 per month, but it provided the extra room that we needed for the soon-to-be five of us. Upon entering the front door, there was a flight of stairs on the side of the house that led straight upstairs. Once upstairs, there was a door that opened the kitchen. Before entering the kitchen, we would bypass the bathroom on the left.

We would enter the kitchen on the right side. The kitchen was larger and had more top and bottom wall cabinets. The kitchen arrangement was a little unusual, but we could live with it. The stove was on one side, and the refrigerator was close to the stove. There were two windows in the kitchen, one on the right side and one on the left side. The sink was on the left side near the window, and the stove was on the right side near the other window. The floor was made of beautiful green tiles with a white-dotted design. The entire apartment walls were painted white. The remainder of the apartment floors were made of beautiful square-shaped wooden parquet flooring. When cleaned, the wooden parquet gave off an exquisite and lasting shine.

Outside the kitchen was a hallway with a linen closet. On the left side of the hallway was the living room, and on the right side were two bedrooms. The living room was quite different from the other apartment. There was a beautiful glass door that led to an outside patio. The glass door was enclosed within a frame with a glass setting. I had to make sure that this door was always locked because of the twins. Kevin, the older twin, would try to go out the door if left unlocked. Kevin was a very mischievous toddler.

Mom bought us some beautiful patio furniture to spruce up our patio. Mom was genuinely gifted in house decor. She taught me numerous simple ideas that made my new home look fabulous. The left side of the living room had a beautiful wall. There were push-up windows with a lock mechanism in the center. I could open the windows to air out the apartment periodically. Mom did most of the decorating. We dressed the windows with eloquent drapes to accent the decorative rugs that we brought with us from the other apartment.

The two bedrooms were side by side on the opposite side of the hallway. In the twins' room, we arranged two beds that will transition from a crib to a toddler bed to a full-sized bed. Since I was pregnant, I kept one of the cribs from the twins and placed it in this room also for our baby on the way. We also placed two chests with drawers for the twins and our baby on the way. We dressed the window in this room with shades to control the outside light and sheer drapes to add some style. The wooden flooring was decked with decorative rugs to provide comfort to the feet.

Our bedroom was right next to our children's bedroom. We were using the same white bedroom furniture that we had brought from the other apartment. We decorated the window in our room with shades and sheer drapes Mom gave us. We accented the wooden flooring with decorative rugs.

We managed to get completely moved in without any problems. God blessed us in finding another apartment and providing good help to make this move. The neighborhood was a middle-class neighborhood with a mix of Germans, blacks, and Italians. The neighborhood was nice and convenient. Almost everything was within walking distance. There was a grocery store, pharmacy, and a shopping center all within a few blocks.

During this pregnancy, James started to pamper me once again. For some reason, pregnancy had a way of bringing out his better qualities. If only he would behave in this manner all the time. I must admit that I truly enjoyed the candy, flowers, and all the romantic gestures that James offered. If only there was a way to transfer this pampering and thoughtfulness beyond the realms of pregnancy. The overall effect could be positive for my marriage. However, James's good behavior was always short lived.

James was still working steady at Kew Gardens in maintenance. I had to stop working because of my pregnancy. It was hard for me because everywhere I went, I had to take the twins with me. This meant I had to take them with me to my doctor's appointments too. The doctor said that I was doing too much. James came with me to the doctor a couple of times. Sometimes James would bathe the twins for me and get them ready for bed while I would wash dishes and clean the kitchen.

Childbirth Number 3

During the middle of one night, I kept going back and forth to the bathroom. About 6:00 a.m., I started to feel cramps in my stomach. I knew I was about to go into labor. About 7:00 a.m., Daddy and Mom came to the house as if they were summoned by God to arrive at that exact needed moment. I was in the bathroom.

Mom told me, "Get out of that bathroom before you have the baby in there." What she said to me made sense. James decided that he should not go to work because I needed to get to the hospital. Mom and Dad took us to the hospital, and I delivered a baby girl about one hour after arriving at the hospital. Daddy always thought babies were ugly, but this one, he said, was very pretty. I ran a fever after childbirth, so I remained in the hospital for seven days. We named our baby girl Angela.

Angela was born on May 2, 1960, and I was about two months shy of my twenty- fourth birthday. Once again, James was excited about the birth of his new daughter. He helped me with almost everything for about two weeks. He would bathe the twins, change diapers, warm bottles, and get up at night for Angela.

Friends from our church gave numerous baby gifts consisting of baby clothing, pink sheets, outfits, and more. At that time, many people believed in old superstitions that you should wait until the baby is born before buying baby gifts. This never really made sense to me, but I did not say anything. Mom and Dad came over often and gave me a break. Dad would tell me to lie down and get some rest while he would feed Angela and the twins, wash the dishes, and clean the kitchen. Sometimes Dad would spend the day cooking food for me and the kids. I always felt like I had one of the best dads in the world. Mom was working but still would come over once or twice a week to help. My parents were extremely helpful when I needed them most.

After about two weeks, James's kindness tapered off. He would bathe the twins, and that was all. I was on my own from that point. He had become as lazy as before. This time was more difficult for me because my body needed to recover from childbirth, and I had to take care of a newborn child and twin toddlers. My doctor told me that I should sleep when the babies are asleep, but how could I when I had other things that I needed to do also.

I had to keep a close eye on the older twin, Kevin. Kevin was quick to get into things if I was not watching him. One day, Kevin took a bobby pin and put it into an electric outlet and slightly burned the tip of his finger. Kevin was also the instigator of the two twins. Kenneth was a little more reserved.

Slowly, I was beginning to adjust to having three children. I had to change my routine and schedule so that I could give each child some time. To do this, I would take one child at a time and place him or her in my lap. While holding Angela, the twins would try to take her out of my lap. They acted like Angela was their baby. Gradually, the twins warmed up to having a baby sister in the home.

James had to be at work by 7:00 a.m. He would wake up between 5:00 a.m. to 5:30 a.m. and would check on the children. If they were crying, he would take care of them. Before James would leave for work, I would get up and take a shower to give me a chance to prepare my day with the children. This was my daily routine for quite some time.

After Angela was about one month old, Mother and Papa Albert came up to visit us. James's behavior started to change back to his old ways. James was still working at the same job. Mother would go and buy food for us. She also made my favorite homemade lemon pies. She cooked us big, delicious dinners. We really enjoyed the excellent meals and all her help.

One day, while Mother and Papa Albert were visiting us, James asked me to bring something to him, but it took me a long time to get it to him. He raised his hand to hit me, and Papa Albert saw him. Papa Albert told him, "If you lay one hand on her, I will kill you!"

Mother rushed in and told Papa Albert, "Stay out of it. This is not our business. Let's try to resolve this peacefully. "Mother knew that Papa Albert carried a gun with him because he worked for the railroad. She was afraid that he would have carried out exactly what he told James. She was trying to immediately diffuse the very tense situation. Slowly, James started to cool down some.

Mother went downstairs to talk to the landlord's wife because we did not have a phone. She asked her to call a cab for them to go to Penn Station as they were going back to Florida that day. Mother talked to the landlord's wife. "Please keep an eye on my child and her children because I do not trust him."

The landlord's wife said to mother, "James was very nasty to me also. He always seems to have an attitude with me." The landlord wife agreed to keep a watchful eye on the situation. The landlord and his wife were very nice people. The wife would cook dinner for us and bring it up to us.

She was a very good cook. Mother and Papa Albert remained a couple more hours before leaving. When the cab arrived, we said our goodbyes. I was very disappointed in James that they had to leave under those circumstances. I was enjoying Mother and Papa Albert's visit.

About two to three months later, I was going to the hair salon to get my hair done. James would not keep the twins and Angela for me, so I had to take them with me. Mom and Dad always paid for me to get my hair done. After leaving the hair salon, James met us and accused me of another man. He raised his hand to hit me, and a lady from the hair salon saw him and told him, "Mister, if you hit her, I will call the police! She does not have a boyfriend. She just got her hair done!" James replied, "You just don't know what you are talking about." James was angry and walked away.

I took my time walking home with my children. I never knew what I would be walking into when I got home. The twins got a little scared. They did not understand why their daddy was hitting their mom.

James accused me a couple more times about having other men. Oftentimes, I was scared of James, but I was more concerned with protecting the children. After Angela was about a year old, I went to the hair salon to get my hair done. James acted the same way as before, accusing me of another man. So, I went home and packed some stuff in a bag and called a cab to take me to Mom and Dad's house. I was planning to leave him for good. James came over every day at mealtime. Mom offered him supper—of course, he did not turn it down.

He started talking to me, saying, "I can't live without you."

I fell for his lines, and a week later, I went back home in a cab.

After we arrived back home, James went to the delicatessen and bought some food for me and the children. He was very nice for a couple of weeks, but again he returned back to his old ways. One day, James asked the twins, "Did one of Mommy's old boyfriends come over to the house?" The twins said, "No." James scared them by yelling at them, "You know someone came over!" Out of fear of their daddy the second time, they said, "Yes." James turned around and struck me right in front of the twins. The twins were scared and did not know what to do. They did not understand why their father was hitting their mommy. That was not the last time that he accused me of another man. This nightmare was ongoing.

Angela was about six months old when James's sister Louise stopped by to visit. She was on vacation visiting Aunt Flo when she asked us if she could take the twins and Angela to see their grandparents in North Carolina. James's parents had never seen the children. Louise asked to take them with her for two weeks. As a typical concerned mother, I asked numerous questions to ensure that our children would receive that same care as at home. "Do you have a washer to wash the children's clothes?"

"Yes, we do. There is no need to worry. They will be well taken care of."

James and I gave her permission to take the children even though I felt a bit reluctant. I had never been without my children.

Three weeks passed, and we heard nothing from Louise. We did not have a phone for her to call us. However, I expected her to at least write us a letter. We had become quite concerned because of the lack of communication, so we asked Daddy to let us borrow the car to go to North Carolina to pick up the children.

When we arrived, Louise told me that she intended to bring the children back the following week but forgot to let us know. I found out that they did not have a washing machine as Louise claimed but instead a clothesline. They also had an outhouse and not a regular bathroom. I did not want my children exposed to this. My children were introduced to the watermelon patch and had eaten so many watermelons that I thought they were going to get sick. The children really enjoyed themselves. I was happy to see my children. I wasn't as happy to hear what Louise's daughter, Shirley said to me as soon as she saw me. She said, "You're pregnant, aren't you?" I was shocked by her statement and was hoping that she was wrong. As we drove back to New York, I was wondering if I was pregnant. I was not ready to have another child.

After we came back home, I went to the doctor, and he confirmed that I was about a month pregnant. It was January 1961, and I am twenty-four and a half years old. Once again, James became excited by the news, and the pampering began once again. He bought me flowers and beautiful cards and more of my favorite things. James would write some very beautiful words to me. He had such beautiful handwriting.

It was hard for me to believe that I was pregnant again. Mom was shocked, and the reaction from my neighbors was the same: "You're pregnant again?"

James's good behavior was once again short-lived. He returned back to his old ways. One time, I was bringing in the garbage cans from outside, and he accused me of seeing the garbage man. He acted badly again and needed to calm down. He left the house and walked to the store. When he came back from the store, he treated me a little better. There were no more incidents throughout the remainder of that pregnancy.

Childbirth Number 4

One Friday, I was in the living room watching television when my water broke. It was good that James came home early that day. James called a cab to go to the hospital. The doctor said this would be hard labor because my water broke and the baby was not ready yet. I spent Friday and Saturday at the hospital. The doctor suggested for me to go home and find something to do to keep busy. So, I went back home and got on my knees and scrubbed all the floors. The baby was born on Sunday, August 13, 1961. James was happy again that he is a proud father of another boy. We named him James Jr. after his father.

Immediately after birth, the doctors told me that James Jr. had a congenital birth disorder called blue baby syndrome. This is a condition in which the heart fails to properly divide into the pulmonary trunk and the aorta. When the heart is developed properly, oxygenated blood is kept separate from deoxygenated blood from the body. This type of defect causes the heart to send out mixed blood through the arteries back to the body. In other words, when the heart does not divide properly, the blood becomes mixed, and the body does not receive the proper oxygen needed.

This can result in a pale bluish color to the skin. If left untreated, blue baby syndrome can be fatal.

The doctor explained the need to perform surgery right away to close up the hole to keep the blood from becoming mixed. James Jr. would also need a blood transfusion to replace the mixed blood in his body. I signed papers to authorize the procedure. The doctor came by after the procedure was completed and told me that the procedure was successful. I was grateful to God for his intervention.

After we received the good news, James bought cigars to pass on to people. Many people at the hospital thought James was such a nice person. They said that he was always bringing me something. They did not know that he was more like Dr. Jekyll and Mr. Hyde.

I had to remain in the hospital seven days again. After seven days, I was released. But James Jr. was kept in the hospital for two more weeks because he was losing too much weight. I became very concerned about the twins' and Angela's health after finding out that James Jr. was born with a congenital heart defect. I had a long conversation with my doctor. I asked him to explain how this happened. My doctor seemed to believe that a combination of my rare blood type and a few other factors may have contributed to the birth defect. I wanted to make sure the twins and Angela did not have any birth defects, so I asked the doctor to thoroughly check for abnormalities. After all the tests were completed, the doctor informed me that no abnormalities were found. I was happy to hear the good news.

After two weeks, James went to the hospital to pick him up and bring him home. I was told that I did not have to come to the hospital. At home, James helped me prepare food. He fed and bathed the children for me. After about two weeks, he went back to his old habits. The twins were then four years old and were able to help me. The twins knew where I kept things such as diapers, lotion, baby bottles, baby oil, and more. The twins would bring these items to me when I asked for them. Mom was still coming around once a week because she was working, and Daddy would come at least twice a week to help me.

At this point, we had four children, and James's income from his job was just a little over one hundred dollars per week. At this point, we could buy a decent amount of food for fifteen dollars, and we had a good amount of help from family and the landlord's wife downstairs. Mom and Dad contributed money and food quite often. Mother and Papa Albert would send us about twenty-five dollars every three months. Uncle Thomas and Aunt Estelle also gave us money at times. Daddy paid rent for us a few times and helped us with milk and continued to pay for diaper service until James Jr. was born.

James continued to behave in an irrational and uncontrollable manner. When he was angry, he would become so enraged about anything that opposed him. Sadly, I was often the victim. When James was raging with anger, most often, he acted in response to what he believed intruded on his territory. Unfortunately, the thing that he believed made the intrusion was simply a delusion.

James was an abusive husband who became extremely jealous of ridiculous things. He would make up things in an attempt to justify his behavior. In public, he would portray a normal pleasant picture of a husband but in private, he was cruel and violent. James often showed little or no regard to me or our children's safety or well-being.

He never accepted responsibility for his repeated destructive behavior. James was verbally and physically abusive. He refused to admit that he had a drinking problem, anger problem, and jealousy problems. Because of James's abusive behavior, I lived in constant fear for myself and my children. I tried to hide numerous physical blows that he inflicted on me.

I was scared of what James would do if he knew that I told someone. I was afraid of what others, especially Daddy, would do to him if they found out. For the most part, I thought if I could somehow hang on, he would change.

When James was in an angry rage, he was a madman. Many times, James would use his fist to punch holes into walls, break furniture, or rip apart fixtures. James gave no regard to the presence of our children. In his rage, he would continue to strike blow after blow to my body in front of our children. He would also verbally abuse me in front of the children. The twins would often try to stop their father from beating me by stepping in between us. James would tell them to go to their room. Once, when the twins jumped in the middle of us, James hit the twins. I believe this occasion was an accident, but James never apologized to the twins.

Majority of James's accusations were infidelity, which were nearly impossible. I never met majority of the men that he accused me of having an affair with because they did not exist. He accused me of having boyfriends in our apartment while he was at work. Oftentimes, James and I would be together, and he would accuse me of men that I had never seen before. On one occasion, a couple was walking past our apartment, and both people spoke to us. Automatically, James would point out that the man was my boyfriend. Some of James's claims were entirely unrealistic. One day, James said that I had a man in the house, and he knew it because he saw footprints on the sidewalk pavement. Go figure!

One day, James was in another violent, angry rage, yelling and inflicting more painful blows on my body. The landlord's wife heard everything downstairs and ran upstairs to my defense. The front door was unlocked, and she ran in and got in between both of us to pull him off of me. She told him, "If you hit her again, I am going to call the police myself. I will personally make sure that you are put away! I will not put up with this anymore. You are going to have to leave. You have thirty days to move out. I am allowing thirty days only because of your wife and children. If my husband was here, he would throw you out right now, and your wife and children would be allowed to stay!" This shook-up James. *Will he take heed and change his behavior?*

The landlord's wife spoke with me separately, saying,

"You do not have to put up with this. I know that you are trying to save your marriage and that you love your husband and hope that he will change. I don't believe that he will ever change."

I was upset. I took what the landlord's wife said to me very seriously. Again, I was thinking about leaving him for good. A short while after, James was talking nice to me again. I saw him playing with the kids as if nothing had happened. I said to myself, *"Maybe I will stay a little longer.*

Once again, because of James, we were forced to move. But this time, we have four children.

CHAPTER 4

171st Street

Once again, God led us to another place to live. I did not understand why my beautiful dream of marriage turned into a never-ending nightmare. However, I can't but notice that God continued to open doors for me and our children.

So, there we were, forced to move because of James's angry tirades. This time, God directed us to the apartment downstairs below Mom and Dad on 171st Street. The thought of being closer to my parents brought me hope.

The downstairs apartment was recently vacated by Mrs. Bell, a good friend of my parents, making this apartment available in ideal timing for us. James used Uncle Herman's truck to move us. Daddy, James, and both of his cousins all helped us move into our next apartment. I helped prepare as much as possible ahead to make our move a smooth one.

The rent at this location was one hundred dollars per month, which is fifty dollars less than our Springfield Gardens apartment. Unfortunately, this apartment did not possess the same modern conveniences as our other apartment. The furnace, the apparatus used to heat the entire house, was located in the basement of this house. There were two furnaces in the basement. One furnace was for our apartment downstairs, and the other furnace was for my parents' apartment upstairs. We used the furnace to heat the house during the colder months and window fans to cool the apartment during the warmer months since we were without air-conditioning. We were responsible for maintaining coal for the furnace. In the apartment that we had just left, the landlord took care of this for both apartments. Whenever we started to run low on coal, we would contact the coal delivery man to deliver more coal to the house. The coal man would bring coal to us via truck. We had a special place in the basement set aside for the coal. Our basement had cellar doors, which opened from the outside of the house directly into the basement. The truck had a chute that was used to deliver the coal from the truck straight to our basement.

We had to make numerous adjustments in this apartment because of the inconveniences due to old fashioned appliances and fixtures. The kitchen was a nice size. It had two pushup windows on each wall. The stove was on one wall, and the refrigerator was sitting against the opposite wall. We placed our China cabinet against another wall. In the kitchen, our sink was designed as a double sink propped up by skinny legs. There was no cabinetry built on or around the sink. This sink was an eyesore, to say the least. The kitchen did not have any cabinets for us to store dishes, pots, or food in. To alleviate this problem, James bought a couple of tall white aluminum cabinets and placed one on each side of the sink. We used these cabinets to store our canned goods and dry foods.

All the appliances were old-fashioned and out-of-date in relation to style. The refrigerator was normal size, but the circular motor located on the top and the legs underneath were a very unpleasant sight. The motor on top of the refrigerator left no room for storing items. The lack of cabinets made cooking and storage difficult and inconvenient. However, James, Mom, and Dad found a way to create a more user-friendly kitchen. The kitchen floor was the only element that did not require any adjustments. The flooring was lined with beautiful black-and-white tiles, which was easy to clean and added a touch of elegance missing in the appliances.

Upon exiting the kitchen, we walked through the hallway that led to the bathroom, bedrooms, and the living room areas. On the left of the hallway was the bathroom. We could exit the bathroom into the hallway or straight into our bedroom. There were stairs that led from the hallway down into the basement. The flooring in our bathroom was lined with beautiful black-and-white square tiles similar to the kitchen floor. The bathroom fixtures were old-fashioned and outdated even for 1962. The toilet was the only bathroom fixture that wasn't outdated. The sink was designed almost the same as the kitchen sink. The only difference was that it wasn't a double sink. It too had skinny propped legs and it had no cabinetry attached for storing items. Our bathtub was a half-oval-shaped container with legs on the bottom. It definitely lacked appeal and the modern look of relaxation. This apartment needed a linen closet. To make up for this deficiency, we placed one of our chests of drawers in the hallway and stored our towels and linens in it.

The bedrooms were smaller than the bedrooms in our previous apartment. In the children's bedroom, we arranged two twin beds, a small juvenile bed, and a crib. Most of the time, I left the crib in the living room. We were also able to fit the three chests of drawers in their room. The flooring throughout the apartment (with the exception of the kitchen and bathroom) was lined with linoleum. Since we were not very fond of some of the colors, James replaced the linoleum color in a few areas. The children's bedroom floor was replaced with blue linoleum flooring.

Our bedroom was located next to the children's bedroom. Our room was too small to fit all our bedroom furniture in. We were only able to fit our bed and our dresser with the matching mirror.

The living room was a reasonable size, and it included a screened porch with mostly windows and some screening enclosures. James replaced the flooring in the living room with blue linoleum with a flowery design. We used the same decorative rugs that we brought with us from the other apartment. The apartment walls were made of sheetrock and painted white.

We did not have a washer and dryer. My parents said that I could use their washer. Since they did not have a dryer, we hung up a clothesline with a roller. The roller made it easy to pull on the clothesline to hang clothes on to dry and remove clothes from the same location. On rainy days, we used the clothesline that we placed in the basement.

As usual, Mom and Dad helped us transition into another apartment. Mom continued to display her natural gifting in home decorating and organizing. I was amazed to see James follow the exact instructions given by Mom in the decorating process. However, most men would leave this up to the wife to sort out. After numerous adjustments and learning how to turn inconvenience into a creative living space, our new home was ready for us to enjoy.

After all of this, James appeared tired from all the physical demands of moving. About four to five months later, I was sitting outside on the front steps when a few of our friends who James and I grew up with stopped by. This was not uncommon for these guys to stop and speak when passing by our place. All of us used to hang out together, James included. These young men were a singing group who recorded professional songs. We talked and laughed for some time until James came home. The guys spoke to James in a very nice manner, but James was unfriendly in his response. James went into the house. After we said good-byes, I came into the house. Immediately, James asked me, "Which one of them is your boyfriend?"

Once again, I tried to make James see how crazy he sounded. James knew these guys as well as I did. I did not want to argue and thank God James did not prolong his jealous tendencies this time.

A few days later, I received a call from Mother. I had to go upstairs to my parents' apartment because we did not have a phone. When I came back downstairs, James asked me, "Was that one of your nig...s?"

"That was Mother calling to inform me that my aunt Corrine's son had just died." I was very upset to hear this bad news. Aunt Corrine was one of Mother's sisters. Her son was only twenty-six years old.

Then James responded, "Oh, I'm sorry." Shortly afterward, he started to calm down.

February 1962, and I'm 26 years old, and I just found out that I was pregnant again. I cannot say that I was excited like James, but I accepted this as God's will. In James's excitement, he started buying gifts for me again. His behavior continued for most of this pregnancy.

Childbirth Number 5

On November 8, 1962, the same day that President Roosevelt's wife died, I went into labor. At 5:00 a.m., I heard the news of her death. While everyone else was, I took a bath, got dressed, and put on my makeup. I told James, "I have to go."

James replied, "Where are you going?"

"To the hospital to have this baby."

James ran upstairs to ask Mom and Dad to stay with the children and for a ride to the hospital. Daddy drove us to the hospital, and Mom stayed with the children until James came back home in a taxi.

I gave birth three hours after arriving at the hospital. We were the proud parents of another boy. He was eight pounds and three ounces. We named him Adam. He was the largest baby that I had given birth to. I asked my doctor to check for congenital birth defects. My doctor informed me that Adam checked out okay. Once again, I had to wait seven days before I was released. I was placed in the maternity ward with two other women who had given birth that day. One woman was Jewish, one was Italian, and I was black. One woman's baby died right after giving birth. The three of us got along extremely well. We each tried to help each other during recovery. After seven days, it was time for me and Adam to come home. Mom and Dad bought a new outfit and receiving blanket for Adam to wear home.

It was still November, and Thanksgiving Day was approaching. We did not have any food or money to buy a Thanksgiving meal. James was out sick from work for about a month, so our finances were far stretched. Daddy bought us our Thanksgiving meal. I cooked roasted chicken, mashed potatoes, green beans and made some Kool-Aid for us to drink. Mom baked a cake for us. Thanksgiving Day turned out much better than expected. I was very grateful to Mom and Dad for providing us with food to eat. God came through for us once again.

On one rare occasion, James asked me to go with him to his job. I asked him, "How can I go to your job, and who will watch the children?" James replied, "I'll get a babysitter to watch the children all night." James contacted a babysitter, Ms. Edna, who was a wonderful lady to watch the children one night for us.

I went with James to his job that night. He asked me to answer the phone calls and take messages for him while he worked. I answered the phone and gave him the messages that I had taken all night. As soon as we came home, James wanted to fight again. He accused me of having another man when I was answering the phone while he was out working. James would never listen to anything reasonable. Eventually he calmed down without prolonging his crazy accusation.

It was March 1963, and once again, I suspected and received confirmation that I was pregnant again. I know that my neighbors will respond the same as before— shocked that I was pregnant again. I never expected to have so many children, but I accept God's will. James became excited again and bought little gifts for me. There was a time that James was late in coming home, and he asked the twins, "Did a man come here today?"

The twins replied, "No."

James then scared the twins and pushed them and asked the same question again.

Out of fear, the twins responded, "Yes."

I was not upset with the twins; I was upset with James for scaring them and forcing them to lie. I was glad that James did not prolong this line of questioning. I believed that James had enough common sense not to touch me while I was pregnant.

Once during my eighth month of pregnancy, I went down to the basement to put coal in the furnace, and James locked me out. I ran out of the basement and up the stairs from the outside to my parents and told Daddy that James locked me out. Daddy went downstairs to talk to James. Daddy asked James, "Why did you lock your wife out?"

James replied, "She shouldn't have left the house!"

Daddy responded, "She went down in the basement to put coal in the furnace. If you don't open that door, I am going to call the police!"

James slammed a dining room chair and broke it. Daddy pushed him down. James raised his hand to beat my dad, but Mom walked in. Daddy told Mom to call the police. When the police arrived, they told me that I did not have to press charges because of the confrontation between Daddy and James. The policeman said that my dad could press charges against James and go to court. Daddy said that he wanted to press charges.

When the scheduled court date arrived, Daddy came to me and said, "I was going to press charges, but I am not going to show up. I am a better man than this. I will continue to pray for him because he needs help. You can leave. You do not have to put up with this. We will help you."

I listened carefully to my dad. I wanted to leave James a number of times, but I feared that if I ever left, James would hunt me down and kill me and the children. I was even more afraid of what James would do to my dad. I loved my daddy. He was a true man of God. He taught me the ways of God in word and by the life he modeled in front of me. I could not bear the thought of something happening to him. My life with James was dominated by excessive abuse and fear brought on by James's erratic and violent behavior toward me. His alcohol abuse only intensified his violent and abusive nature.

Daddy did not show up just as he told me, and James found out in court. James came home and ran upstairs and apologized to Daddy. Daddy forgave him and said to James, "You need the Lord, James!"

"You are a good man. I used to go to church faithfully, but I don't know what happened to me," James responded.

Daddy immediately replied, "You are the man of your house. You need to take your wife and children to church."

"I will."

Of course, this never happened. The only time that James went to church was for a funeral. After this incident, James calmed down for about one month or so.

Childbirth Number 6

On the morning of December 26, 1963, I went into labor. I decided to bathe, get dressed, and put on my makeup. I told James, and he wanted to know where I was going all dressed up. I told him I was going to the hospital to have the baby. I gave birth two to three hours after arriving at the hospital. I delivered a baby girl weighing six pounds, five ounces. We named her Juliet. Immediately after Juliet was born, my doctor informed me that she was born with the same congenital heart defect that James Jr. was born with. She too was a blue baby and needed to have the same procedure performed on her heart. The procedure was successful. I was so grateful to God for guiding the hands of the doctors performing the procedure. I was able to bring Juliet home with me after seven days.

Almost everyone commented on her big baby legs. At that time, Adam was still in diapers and just learning to walk. The twins were six years and eight months old and were very helpful to me. James Jr. was potty trained and ate some table food.

Right after Juliet was born, Mom and Dad moved out from upstairs into a house on 207th Street. I was happy that they now have a house with more space, but I was a little sad that they were no longer in the same building.

Juliet was about five to six months old when James became antsy again. He started to voice his need for some fresh air. Of course, this really meant that he wanted to go to the bar to drink. Since he acted as if going out was so important, he left to hang out with the boys. Shortly afterward, James returned home looking very ragged and angry. He looked like someone physically got the best of him. He did not want to talk about it, but it was apparent that someone beat him up. I wondered what James did to provoke such a beating. He started to let off steam and frustration by punching a hole in the crib that Juliet was sitting in. Immediately, I ran and grabbed her from the crib before James inflicted serious bodily harm to his own daughter. I left the room to allow him to calm down. I was always trying to protect my children from James's angry tirades. It was Sunday, and I had just finished cooking dinner. The children were eating in the kitchen and James and I were eating in the living room when we heard a car horn blowing. James yelled out, "That must be your boyfriend!" I responded, "How many times do I have to tell you that I do not have a boyfriend?"

Before I could blink my eyes, James slapped me across the face so hard that he caused my nose to start bleeding, and he broke the plate in my hand.

Aunt Flo came in and saw my face and yelled at him, "I can't believe that you are beating your wife. You need to straighten up, or I will call the police! I just came by to tell you that your mother just died."

The news of his mom's death shook him up. James started crying. I have a bloody nose, and I'm in pain, but I placed his grief above the intense physical pain that he just inflicted on me. I came over to console him. After a little time, he started to calm down. A little later, James ran upstairs and asked Daddy if he could borrow the car for us to go to North Carolina to attend his mother's funeral. Daddy granted his permission, and our parents agreed to watch the children while we were away.

We drove to North Carolina to his parents' house. There were so many people in the house, so we slept on the couch. The next day, his sisters and brothers were arguing, and James tried to calm them down. He told his siblings, "You don't need to be fussing. Mom's dead!" Who would've ever imagined that James would act as a family mediator?

On Saturday, we rode together to the funeral with Aunt Flo, Aunt Lucille, and Uncle Fred. The funeral was very sad. Many people were weeping intensely.

On Sunday, we drove back to New York. The drive was approximately an eight-hour trip. We were exhausted when we arrived home, but I was happy to see our children. I did not like being away from my children. My children are a wonderful blessing from God. This was the only bright spot in my marriage that I felt joy.

Childbirth Number 7

James's behavior was good for about three to four months. Within that time, I found out that I was pregnant again. I don't fully understand why I am having so many children, but this must be God's will. I must admit that I love my children deeply from the moment that I first lay eyes on them.

James was excited and treated me very nicely for a short while. He started a few arguments, always about a man, but he did not try to prolong his accusations. When we went out, people thought that we were one of the nicest couples. James's personality in public was far better than his personality at home. Dr. Jekyll and Mr. Hyde syndrome come to mind here. James was calm until I gave birth again. On April 04, 1965, four hours after arriving at the hospital, I gave birth to another baby girl. She was seven pounds, and we named her Jennifer. I was not given anything for pain for this delivery. My delivery was completely natural this time. I asked my doctor to thoroughly check Jennifer for congenital birth defects. He informed me that she checked out okay. I thank God for blessing me with another healthy baby.

We were the parents of seven children. The twins were eight years old, and they enjoyed helping me around the house. Angela was five years old, James was almost four years old, Adam was almost three years old, and Juliet was a year and a half. We had a full house, and James's income has not increased.

Shortly after Jennifer was born, James lost his job. When I asked James how he lost his job, he replied, "My boss called me in the office and told me, 'We do not need you anymore. We do not have enough funds to continue paying you.'" As a result, James filed for unemployment.

We were already struggling financially. James had fallen behind two months with our rent before he lost his job. Unemployment insurance was not enough for us to survive on. We had to rely more and more on my parents for financial help. After James's unemployment insurance ran out, I applied for public assistance. At that point, we were about four months behind on our rent, and we had received an eviction notice. Public assistance provided us with food stamps and a monthly check. I was grateful that public assistance also paid the landlord all our back rent to make us current. James said that he was looking for work, but he wasn't really looking. After we started receiving help from the public assistance, James became comfortable and very lazy. He was enjoying the benefits without having to work for it.

It was a normal procedure for a public assistance representative to come to the home to verify there was an actual need for assistance. When the public assistance representative arrived at our home, he looked at our household items, and he checked to see what items the children lacked. He asked me questions such as, "How many changes of sheets do you have for the children?

How many blankets, sheets, towels, pots, pans, dishes, and kitchen items do you have?"

I answered all of his questions, and then he walked through the apartment to confirm my answers and verify actual need.

He told me, "You need many things for both of you and your children. I will expedite funds to you so that you can go and buy these things."

We received the check as promised, and I went to the store and bought all the items that he told me to buy. It was very important for me to follow his instructions. I bought sheets, towels, bedspreads, blankets, pots, pans, tablecloths, dishes, and so on.

The representative came back and was pleased with how well I followed his instructions. The representative told me that we needed more space for the children. Public assistance helped provide a real estate agency to locate a larger place for us to live. The agency found a larger apartment for us in Brooklyn. We were very grateful for the help that public assistance provided for us. The help did not stop at that point. After about two months, public assistance arranged for a moving truck and a crew who packed our belongings, loaded the truck, and unloaded the truck at the new place for us. Wow, I was almost speechless. This was truly the hand of God working in our favor.

CHAPTER 5

Brooklyn Move

Moving this time was so much easier than all our previous moves. Thank God for placing the right people in the right places at the most-needed times. The movers were very professional, and they eliminated all logistical worries. Our main concern was determining bedroom assignments and arranging the furniture and decor. We were fortunate to be allowed to clean our new apartment before the move-in date. Previously, we would have to clean the apartment *after* moving all our furniture in. Apartments were not always very clean at move-in time. I was glad that I could mop the floors and clean the windows beforehand.

There we were, moving into a large four-bedroom, one-bathroom apartment. This was the largest apartment that we've had so far. This apartment is located in Brooklyn, New York, approximately eighteen miles from our 171st Street apartment. It was another upstairs apartment, but we were very pleased with the spacious living arrangement of this place. Four bedrooms provided more breathing space for the children. We could no longer keep all the children in one bedroom while we used the other bedroom. We had outgrown two-bedroom living. It was July 1965, about three months after giving birth to my seventh child, Jennifer, and we have just moved into our fourth apartment.

I was quite pleased with our new place for several reasons. This apartment had four bedrooms, a larger kitchen, and wall cabinets for storage in both the kitchen and the bathroom. Both tenants had a key to the main door located at the front of the house.

Entering this apartment was similar to our previous apartment. Upon entrance into the house, we would take the flight of stairs to the right of the downstairs apartment to go upstairs. A small foyer was located opposite our kitchen door. The only entrance into our apartment was through the kitchen door. This kitchen was large enough for placement of our table and chairs and our China cabinet. The extra space in the kitchen made up for the lack of a dining room. The floor was lined with beautiful black-and- white large square tiles.

The two push-up windows were situated on the side walls opposite each other. One window faced our next-door neighbor's apartment without impeding on our privacy.

To my pleasure, the stove, refrigerator, and sink were much more updated. Cabinetry was built beneath the double sink for storage. No more unsightly skinny prop legs. I was delighted that we did not have to make any adjustments to remedy cabinet space in this apartment. Overall, the enormous workspace was a blessing.

We could exit the kitchen by either veering to the right to go directly into the living room or veering left and enter directly into the bathroom. The living room was located on the front side of the house. This room was very large and lined with wooden flooring and two push-up windows.

We dressed the windows with drapes and centered our decorative rugs under the coffee table to highlight the furniture colors and bring balance to the room. We did not have a patio in this apartment like our previous place, but this did not detract from the look and spacious rooms.

Because of public assistance, we were able to purchase new living room furniture. We bought a black sofa, two regular chairs, and a coffee table with a glass top. James built two maple-tan colored end tables to match our maple coffee table. Our nineteen-inch television sat on top of a small stand in the living room. We were limited to black-and-white television viewing for entertainment. Color television was still quite new with only a few stations airing in color.

We have just one bathroom, but we seem to efficiently manage its use. Our bathroom was located to the left of the kitchen. This bathroom was larger than the one in our last apartment. The flooring was lined with very small white tiles, the same as the white tiles on the wall. Our bathtub was a white cast iron design propped on top of four claw foot pedestals. We have not yet experienced a modern built-in bathtub with waste drains, hot and cold-water taps, and an overhead shower. Nevertheless, life moves on.

The sink in this bathroom is up to date with built-in cabinets below for storage. We were fortunate to have a medicine cabinet located above the sink. Our bathroom lacked a linen closet; however, there were three shelves built directly over the commode. These shelves were useful for the placement of towels and sheets.

As for the bedrooms, one bedroom was located on the left side of the living room in the front of the house. This was the twins' bedroom; it was the only bedroom lined with wooden flooring. The twins' room had two twin beds and one chest of drawers. At the back of the house was the largest bedroom. We gave this room to all three girls because of the size. We were able to place two twin beds, a crib, and a chest of drawers in this room. The girls could exit the kitchen straight into their room. They could also exit their room straight into our bedroom from the other side. Our bedroom was large enough for us to place our bed, dresser and mirror, and tall chest of drawers without feeling cluttered.

On the left side of our bedroom was another bedroom, where we placed two twin beds and a chest of drawers in. We gave this room to James Jr. and Adam. The girls' room, our room, and James Jr. and Adam's room were all located on the back side of the apartment. Each of these three rooms was lined with linoleum flooring. All four bedrooms had a long mirror mounted on the door, a closet, and one push-up window excellent for fresh air. We added a little decor in each room by adding drapes, decorative rugs, and cotton bedspreads.

We were able to purchase additional furniture for the bedrooms from the money we received from public assistance. The extra bedrooms provided more breathing space for us and the children. The twins were excited to have their own room with more space. Angela also seemed content with her new surroundings.

The twins were now eight years old and were transferred from a school in Jamaica to a school in Brooklyn. They were a little nervous at first because they did not know any other kids, but they made new friends shortly afterward. It was not long before the twins became acclimated to their new school and environment. The younger twin, Kenneth, was identified as very intelligent. The school contacted me, asking to advance Kenneth one grade higher. I refused to allow the grade advancement because I did not want Kenneth to leave Kevin behind. It was a year later that I received the same request to advance the older twin, Kevin. Later, I wished that I had allowed Kenneth to advance one grade.

Angela was five years old and started kindergarten. There was a little boy in Angela's class who fell in love with her. He was so crazy about Angela that he told his mother to make sure she makes an extra lunch for Angela also. This was not the only little boy who fell in love with Angela. When Angela was in prekindergarten (pre-K) at four years old, another little boy would often give Angela money. Most of the time, he gave her a quarter, but to Angela, this was a lot of money.

Since James Jr. was four years old, I placed him in pre-K in Brooklyn. At that time— it was August 1965—Adam was a few months shy of his third birthday, Juliet was about one year eight months old, and Jennifer was only three months old.

Shortly after moving in, I began to meet some of our neighbors. One day, I was walking to the grocery store, and a lady, a neighbor, introduced herself and her children to me. Her name was Mrs. Holmes. She and I both had seven children who were about the same ages. Mrs. Holmes asked me if I was born in New York, and I told her that I was born in Florida. I told her that she probably never heard of a small town called Palatka. To my surprise, she told me that she was born in Putnam Hall, Florida, which was about twenty- one miles from

Palatka. We became very good friends. We both cooked and shared food with each other, and our children played together.

There were other women in the neighborhood that I met, but I did not socialize with the other women like I did with Mrs. Holmes. One neighbor, a lady who lived on the right side of our apartment, was very difficult to get along with. She and her five or six children caused numerous problems with others. This lady had picked a fight with all the women in the neighborhood except me. Most of the women would sit outside in front of their houses and gossip about other people. I chose not to participate in this behavior.

On one occasion, this same lady, the instigator, continued in her malicious behavior, creating havoc among the other women. The instigator refused to stop yelling ridiculous statements and cursing at everyone. One of the ladies decided that she was going to put a stop to her madness by going over to her house to fight. One woman's dress was lifted up in embarrassment, and a wig was pulled off. The fight was in progress. The teenagers in the neighborhood and a couple of adults swarmed around this fight as excited fans cheering on their favorite fighter. There was no referee in sight, and a bell could not be heard to end the rounds.

A knockout blow would have brought in the law but no peace. The scene was ugly and embarrassing to say the least. Eventually, a sane adult came and broke up the fight, calling the fight out of order. The fans were ordered to go home, and the two women were reprimanded about their behavior.

The excitement did not stop here. One day, my youngest twin, Kenneth, went to take on the instigator's daughter who fought with most of the neighborhood kids. Other kids called her ugly and picked on her, but she did not back down to anyone. There were a group of kids who came cheering and urging a fight. The day that the fight was scheduled turned out as a rainy day, so the fight never took place. I was glad that the fight did not happen because I did not want my children behaving in a manner like the instigator or her children. Her children's behavior was as awful as their mother's behavior. The common denominator in nearly every neighborhood conflict was either the mother or her children. James's abusive behavior alone was already a frightening situation.

I continued my friendship with Mrs. Homes. I was grateful to have someone to talk to. There were so many horrible things happening in my life, most of which I kept to myself. We talked about many of the terrible things that were happening near us and around the country. We shared our hopes and dreams of leaving Egypt and finding a land flowing with milk and honey. Of course we did not know how this would ever happen.

James's violent and disruptive behavior continued. The children and I were living in a constant state of terror. We were unable to find that "thing" that would set James off in order to avoid it. From day to day, we did not know if it would be our last day. Oftentimes, James could not distinguish between reality and fantasy. His behavior at times appeared consistent with paranoia. Numerous times James claimed that someone was out to get him. He would close the windows and doors, pull down the shades, and demand total silence. James would not allow the children to even whisper. He did not trust anyone and constantly accused the children and me for his delusions.

It was about three to four weeks after we moved in when Mom called the Office of Children and Family Services (OCFS) to report James's abusive behavior. Mom was very concerned that our safety was seriously at risk. She felt that James's behavior could be consistent with a mental disorder. Mom talked to a case worker who said that she would send a psychiatrist to our home to conduct an evaluation of James. She gave Mom the psychiatrist's name so that Mom and I would know who he was when he arrived. This information was kept from James. The case worker assured us that the psychiatrist would not present himself as a psychiatrist but as a representative making a routine visit.

The day of James's psychiatric evaluation had arrived, and the psychiatrist arrived as scheduled. The psychiatrist introduced himself as a representative working for OFCS. He stated that he was asked by a case worker to conduct a random interview of the family.

The psychiatrist started asking questions. Most of the questions were directed to James to answer. He started by asking, "Is everyone happy in the family?"

James replied, "Yes."

The psychiatrist then asked, "Are the children happy at school?"

"Yes."

"Do you participate in the children's homework?"

"Yes, sometimes."

The psychiatrist continued his general line of questions, with James responding to mostly truthful responses. The next line of questions was directed towards employment. The psychiatrist asked, "Are you working?"

"No, I am unemployed."

"Are you looking for work?"

"Yes, I have been looking for work, but every time I try to look for work, I get sick."

"When was the last time that you looked for work?"

"It was just this week that I went out to look for work, and I got sick."

James was not telling the truth. He was not looking for work. He had become comfortable with receiving food stamps and public assistance monthly checks.

The psychiatrist went on to stress the importance of continuing to look for work and to not giving up. The psychiatrist continued, "What is your highest educational level completed, and what were your areas of study in school?"

"I did not go back to school after I completed the eleventh grade. I did not have a specific course of study."

The interview continued with the psychiatrist with more questions directed to James. "There are reports of you beating your wife. Is this true?"

Immediately, James responded, "I don't know where that statement came from. I have never touched my wife!"

I knew that James was lying, and I wanted to interject so badly, but the psychiatrist winked at me to keep quiet. My interjection would have blown his cover.

"Have you ever taken a drink of alcohol to maybe unwind after a long day?"

"I do take a sip of alcohol only when I can't sleep."

It was difficult to listen to James lie and not say anything, but I did not want to ruin the interview. There were times in which I was curious if James was suffering from a mental disorder or if his violent behavior was a result of severe alcohol abuse.

There were other questions that were asked during this interview. The psychiatrist also made a few more visits before concluding with his assessment of James. After the first visit James asked me, "Why would the representative ask me if I had ever touched you before?" "James, people have seen the way you have treated me in public. Anyone of them could have called and reported your behavior."

After a number of visits, the psychiatrist wrote his report. In his report, he very clearly stated that something was clearly not right with James, and he needed serious help. The psychiatrist stated that he did not know how we could get him help. During this time, a person would have to voluntarily admit himself into an institution or ask for help to receive treatment. The psychiatrist could not treat James without James's permission. This of course posed a problem for the agency to establish the help that James badly needed. Keep in mind that James was in complete denial that he had any problems.

OCFS and the psychiatrist decided to go directly to James, confront him, and talk him into accepting help. The psychiatrist was very direct with James. He did not sugarcoat the effects of James's behavior on me and the children. Great efforts were made to get James to cooperate, but the outcome was unsuccessful. I was very disappointed in the end. This meant that my hope of obtaining help just flew out the window.

What was I to do now? I have suffered repeated violent blows to my body from James. I have hidden this from so many people because of James's unpredictability. I was concerned about my life, the life of my children, and my dad's life. My children and I lived in constant fear. It was bad enough that James was beating me, but he also started beating the twins as if they were adults. The twins would jump in between the two of us to try to protect me from James. This scared me because James would take huge swings, whacking the twins to the floor. I would yell at him and try to protect them from their father. I was always afraid for them. I feared that one day someone maybe be killed, one of us or James. I did not want James's blood on my hands or on my children's hands.

At a much later date, both twins were asked by their sister Juliet how they viewed their father. Their responses were similar. Kenneth said this about his father:

> "His erratic mood swings were unbearable and unpredictable. I felt like we were living on a landmine, and the least little trigger point would set him off. A great percentage of the time we were either walking on pins and needles or eggshells. His anger was out of control. He was a beast to live with, and I felt that we all had to live in such a way to placate his erratic mood swings and swings of violence. To be slapped to the floor is unreal. Hence, I never felt that we had a normal family. I lived with the thought that if we did not get out of this quagmire, somebody was going to be killed."

Kevin described living with his father as:

> "Feelings of emotional terror night after night. I would go to sleep at night hoping to not wake up."

This was not what I imagined my marriage to turn into. What happened to all the promises James made before we got married? He promised to never lay a hand on me and to take care of me. Instead, he beats me repeatedly and our children. The children and I are in a battle called survival.

Women who are abused by their husbands do not have any protection under the law. A husband can beat a woman almost to death, and the police will not take him to jail. However, if one spouse kills the other, that spouse will be taken to jail and charged with murder. The police will threaten the husband to stop, or they will take him to jail, but never will. The law during this time viewed a dispute or fight between husband and wife as mere domestic abuse. There wasn't any law on the books during the 1960s to arrest a husband for beating his wife. The only recourse was to leave and seek help in a shelter.

I wanted to leave James several times. I knew that if I ever left James, he would hunt us down the way animals hunt their prey. I feared for our children. I felt trapped.

I have an aunt, my mother's sister, who was beaten so many times by her husband that she fled. She fled to Buffalo, but he found her and beat her. She fled again to Palatka, and he found her and beat her. She fled to Miami, and he found her and beat her. She fled the last time to Rochester and was at her nephew Chester's house, and her husband came there with a knife. Chester saw the knife. My aunt's husband came towards Chester with the knife and Chester shot him in the leg to stop him. Both men were arrested and taken to jail. Chester was released immediately, but my aunt's husband remained in jail for a long time.

After a long time, he became sick and eventually died. This event was the only thing that seemed to stop him. This is what I fear from James.

For now, I continue to pray even though I feel my prayers are not getting through to God. James had a best friend named Lloyd. Lloyd and his wife, Josephine, were good friends of ours. They lived in Jamaica and would come to visit us in Brooklyn quite often. One day, Josephine and I were sharing things about our husbands with each other. Josephine spoke highly of her husband but was shocked at what I shared about James.

She responded, "James is such a nice man."

I told her, "Do not be fooled by his behavior in front of you. He is a totally different person behind closed doors."

It was difficult to have a relationship with anyone because of James's unpredictable and sometimes embarrassing behavior. There were a number of times that our friends would come over for a visit, and James's attitude would change at any time. You could tell by the expression on his face that he did not want to be bothered. He would never openly verbalize a reason for his change in attitude. Sometimes James would just get up and leave while our friends were still visiting us. He would not say good-bye as a courtesy to our guests.

After pulling this type of stunt a few times, our friends started cutting their visits short. They could have easily stopped coming over, but I believe that they continued coming because of me. Living with James was more difficult each day. Every effort to bring something good or normal into my life, James found a way to disrupt it or destroy it. James did not want other people to see his true character. This would have ruined the good husband's act that he displayed in front of people outside of our home.

CHAPTER 6

Adam

November 1965, and it had been four months since we moved to Brooklyn. It was early evening, and we were all sitting at the dinner table. The children were laughing and playing when I looked across the table and noticed a lump on Adam's neck. Immediately, I got up and walked over to Adam to get a closer look. It wasn't too large, but definitely noticeable. I placed my hands on Adam's neck and felt the knot. It felt hard, but Adam did not seem bothered by the pressure I placed on it. My first thought was this might be the mumps. I knew that swelling on the side of the face was a common symptom with the mumps. Adam did not complain of any pain in his neck. I told James and showed it to him. I told James that I wanted to take Adam to the doctor to have it checked. James agreed that I should take him.

The next day, I dressed Adam and took him to the doctor. The doctor examined him and told me that he would run some tests. A nurse came and drew some blood to run blood work. After the doctor completed his examination, he told me that it appears as though the problem was his lymph nodes. He promised to contact me as soon as the results come back. The doctor wrote a prescription for medicine to give to Adam by mouth for about a week.

Upon arrival back home, I immediately started giving Adam his medicine as instructed by the doctor. I kept a close eye on him to see if there were any changes in the appearance of the knot and for any reactions to the medication. I also checked on him throughout the night.

I regularly checked on the children during the night because of James's unpredictable behavior. Adam's behavior remained unchanged. He played with the other children in the same manner as before. One week had passed and everything looked good. The medicine seemed to be working. The next doctor's visit was scheduled for three weeks from the first visit.

After three weeks, I took Adam to his second doctor's appointment. The doctor examined the knot again and said it looked like the knot shrunk a little. This time, the doctor changed Adam's medicine to something different. He told me to let him know if there were any problems. Adam and I went back home, and I gave him the new medicine as instructed. James asked how the doctor's visit was, and he wanted to know what the doctor said. I told him that the doctor said it looked like some shrinkage had taken place. I also told James that the doctor changed his medicine.

I did not notice anything different in Adam's mood or behavior until about the second day. Adam started throwing up. It looked like a bad reaction from the medicine. Immediately, I contacted the doctor's office, and the doctor changed his medicine back to the original medicine. I didn't have to take him back for a visit until the next scheduled appointment six weeks later. I went back to giving Adam the original medicine, and his throwing up ceased.

I continued to monitor Adam very closely. He seemed happier after going back to the original medicine. There weren't any more reactions to the medicine, and it didn't seem like the knot was growing any larger.

Six weeks had passed; I took Adam to his third appointment. The doctor examined him again and told me to continue giving him the same medicine. Adam's status appeared unchanged. The next appointment was scheduled for two months later. I took Adam back home and continued to keep an eye on Adam's neck and his overall health. James would not go with me to take Adam to the doctor with Adam, but he always wanted to be kept abreast of Adam's condition.

Mom and Dad were very supportive in helping me with the children. Sometimes Mom would come over and watch the children so that I could take Adam to his appointments. If Mom or Dad were not available, I would take all our children with me. James would not help me out by watching the children so that I could take Adam to his doctor's appointment. It would have been nice if I had had some help from James, but he seemed useless in this effort.

James favored Adam over the other children. I did not understand this because he never offered to come with me or take him to any of his visits. However, there were times that he would dress Adam in a cute outfit and a cap and take Adam with him on walks and leave the rest of the children at home. I could understand it if he wanted to take all the boys to the park, but that was not the case. He only wanted Adam, and I believe the other children noticed it. James was doing this before I discovered the knot on Adam's neck. I was a little concerned about this because I did not want any one of our children to feel they received less love and attention than the others. I made it a point to include all the children in activities and made sure that I spent time with each child.

It was late December 1965, about two months since I discovered the knot on Adam's neck. I received a letter from Mother that she was coming to visit for two weeks. I was looking forward to Mother's visit. I really missed her. I realize that Mother will be on vacation, but it will be wonderful to have her help.

The day arrived for Mother's visit, so I got dressed and caught the subway train to meet her. Mother almost always travels by train. She was never fond of flying. I met Mother at Penn Station, and we both caught the subway back to our place. The children were happy to see her.

Mother was an amazing cook and would automatically take the initiative to help out whenever she saw a need. She would go to the store and buy food and cook it for us. I was grateful for any help that I received with taking care of our children. Getting help from Mother was an added benefit because I knew that my children were in good hands, and they loved her dearly. With all the pain inflicted on the children and me by James, having Mother here was a welcoming breath of fresh air.

Mother was very helpful as expected. She was a tremendous blessing to me and the children. We all enjoyed the delicious home-cooked meals and mouthwatering desserts. James enjoyed the food as much as we did. I was surprised but glad that James kept his behavior in check. For once, James was not so hateful to Mother. On all her previous visits, James displayed a nasty attitude toward Mother.

I really enjoyed having Mother around. We went shopping together, and she bought food and clothes for the children. The children loved the special attention and the new clothes. They didn't get to see their grandmother from Florida too often but loved her when she came. Adam loved Mother. He would sit on her lap and give her kisses the same way as he would when I watched television. He was a very affectionate little boy.

Mother and I got the chance to sit at the table and talk about a number of things. During one of our conversations, Mother noticed the knot on Adam's neck and started asking me about it. I told her that I noticed the knot about two months ago. I informed her that I took Adam to the doctor the day after I saw the knot and told her everything the doctor did and told me to do.

Mother was still very concerned about the knot. She did not feel comfortable with the way it looked. She explained that this was not the first time that she had seen similar situations involving people with unusual knots. She was even more concerned because each of the situations that she knew about resulted poorly. "You need to take him back to the doctor. This knot just doesn't look good to me," Mother said.

"Okay, I will," I responded.

I was able to get Adam seen by the doctor again within a couple of days. The doctor said the knot looked about the same. He also said he still thinks it's his lymph nodes.

I brought Adam back home after his doctor's visit, and I explained what the doctor told me to Mother and James. I told them that there wasn't much change from the last examination. I was told to continue giving the medicine and let the doctor know if anything happens. I continued to keep a close eye on Adam, and we enjoyed the remaining time with Mother. When the time came for Mother to go back to Florida, the children and I were sad to see her leave.

Two months had passed, and I took Adam to his regular scheduled doctor's appointment. The doctor thoroughly examined Adam again. This time the doctor said the knot was larger than the last visit. He ordered more blood work and ran more tests to see if the lymph nodes were growing.

The doctor also said this growth situation was progressive but could be treated. He tried to reassure me by saying that Adam could have a long life. He said the medicine should either slow the growth down or stop it completely.

About one month after Adam's last doctor's appointment, he started getting sick. Adam was throwing up and had developed diarrhea. Two weeks later, he was running a fever and throwing up again. I took him to the hospital, and he was admitted because of the fever. The doctor kept Adam in the hospital for about a week to treat him. When it came time for me to leave, Adam was crying because he did not want me to leave. It was hard for me to leave him, but I knew that I had to take care of the other children also.

I went to visit Adam each day that he was in the hospital. On days that I could not get someone to watch the children; I brought all of them with me to the hospital. The hospital had a special room designed for children to hang out and play. There was someone on staff who would watch the children in this room so that the parents could visit their other sick children. The staff were extremely nice to me. They would also feed the children for me. I would come down and spend time with the rest of my children so that they would not feel neglected. After a week, Adam was released. After leaving the hospital, Adam seemed happy and was playing as he normally would.

It was April 1966, and I just found out that I am pregnant again. James of course is happy to hear the news. I don't understand why he gets so excited each time I become pregnant. It's not his body morphing into an unrecognizable figure. Pregnancy places a great amount of demand on my body. I have had difficulty recovering after previous pregnancies because the babies took so much out of me. I battled anemia, fatigue, and weight loss because of pregnancy. I love each one of my children dearly. I place their lives as a priority over my own life. I have an enormous amount of pressure on me with seven children, and I can barely get him to help me with them. James's excitement about having a child on the way was always short-lived, and then I am left with the entire load by myself. It's bad that he refuses to look for a job. There was a time that James was a hard worker, but now he was lazy and too comfortable receiving unearned benefits called public assistance.

Three weeks after Adam was released from the hospital, he got sick again. He was running a fever, shaking from the chills, and was throwing up again. I rushed him back to the hospital. This time the doctor kept him for a couple of weeks for treatment.

Adam was beginning to learn his way around the pediatric ward that he was on. The staff had started spoiling him. The nurses showed him where all the treats for the children were located. Adam really liked the special treatment from the nurses. Adam was given a new name, Errand Boy. He was responsible for passing out the treats to the other sick children, and he loved his new job.

Adam was becoming acclimated to his temporary home away from home. When it was time for me to go home, Adam did not cry anymore. He would walk me to the elevator and kiss me goodbye and then walk back to his room. Each time that I came to visit, Adam would get excited. As soon as he saw me, he would say, "There goes my mommy! I am so happy to see you."

I continued to go back and forth to the hospital to visit Adam. I would spend nearly the entire day with him. Mom and Dad were extremely supportive in dealing with Adam's illness and my need for help with the other children. Many times, Mom and Dad would pick up the twins and keep them for several days at a time. They would take them to church, treat them, and buy clothes and other items as needed. The twins loved going to their grandparents' house.

This was a safe, warm Christian home that my children could exhale and grow in a loving environment. James turned our home into a prison environment full of fear and anger. I was grateful for parents who loved my children and displayed the love of Christ in them. All our children loved their grandparents. They were always excited to see them and spend time with them. After a couple of weeks, Adam was released to go home. He looked good, and his skin color was so beautiful to me.

I continued to check on Adam day and night. One night, I went to check on Adam, and he felt warm to me. He was running at a temperature of 100 °F, so I placed cold compresses on him, and his temperature eventually went down.

I was glad that his temperature went down this time, but I was worried because Adam kept getting sick. I was more curious about Adam's condition. The doctors continued to tell me that Adam has a lymph node condition. I realized that I was not a doctor, and I do not understand much medical jargon, but I was beginning to feel that there was more going on than what was being told to me. From what I could see, Adam's condition was getting worse, not better. He was spending more time in the hospital than at home.

Adam always enjoyed playing with the other children. When he was not sick, Adam was lovable, strong, and very playful. Adam called the twins "Booshum, Baashum." To this day I do not know how he came up with this name. James Jr. and Adam shared rooms together, so it was only natural that the two of them would play together often.

When the boys played together, they enjoyed wrestling against each other on the floor. From time to time, I would have to remind them to not to play so rough. One day Kenneth, James Jr., and Adam were playing around a little too rough on the platform area on the top of the stairs.

It looked like James Jr. was trying to push Adam down the stairs, but Kenneth and Adam were playing a little rough, and Adam accidentally pushed Kenneth and both Kenneth's and Adam's head hit the radiator. Kenneth had a little knot on his head, but it did not bleed. But Adam's head bled. Kenneth was okay, but I was unable to stop the bleeding coming from Adam's head. I quickly asked Mrs. Holmes from downstairs to watch the children so that I could take Adam to the emergency room. I took the city bus while holding his head in my hand.

When we arrived, Adam was taken in immediately because of the bleeding. Adam's doctor came up to me and said, "I'm glad that you got him to the hospital right away. I did not want him bleeding a lot." I wasn't quite sure what he meant by this statement. I was very concerned about my son. The doctor was able to stop the bleeding and was admitted into the hospital.

After a week, Adam was released. He was so happy to be back at home. After about a month, Adam got sick again. I had to take him back to the doctor. As we walked into the doctor's office, Adam said, "This looks just like Grandma's house." The doctor's office was so clean that it reminded Adam of how clean his grandma kept her house. It's amazing the way Adam was able to identify similarities in detail between two different places.

The doctor said, "We have to admit him again." Now I am more confused and upset. I do not understand why Adam kept getting sick. I suspected that there was more going on here than I was told.

I responded in a very strong tone, "Why are you not telling me what is wrong with my child? Adam keeps getting sick, and I need to know why."

"He has leukemia. He may last three months, or he may last a year."

Immediately I asked the doctor, "Why didn't you tell me this before?"

"We were doing everything that we could to save him. I didn't tell you because I didn't want to give you false hope if things didn't work out.

"I felt there was something more than a lymph nodes condition," I said.

A few things started running through my mind. I did not know how to respond to what I just heard. I wanted to know the truth, but how do I swallow the truth when it meant that my child's life was near the end. *How do I break this news to James?* How did this happen? Why Adam? Why now? I don't completely understand leukemia, but I know that it could be terminal.

After spending the rest of the day with Adam at the hospital, I kissed Adam good night and went home. I am physically tired, mentally exhausted, and very heartbroken about Adam's illness. I broke the news to James about Adam. He was hurt when I told him that Adam had leukemia. I could tell by the look on James's face that this was not what he wanted to hear. Both of us believed the doctor was keeping something from us. The fact that the knot on his neck was growing larger and Adam kept getting sick had to mean there was something else happening.

After such a long day and finding out the truth about Adam's illness, I still have the other children to care for. James hadn't offered once to give me a break or to come with me. Instead, James went out the same night and bought a bottle of alcohol and got drunk. Our son was lying in a hospital bed sick with leukemia, and James opted to get drunk. He never considered taking some of the pressure off of me. *Tomorrow, I will go back to the hospital and take our children while James sits home.* My children are a blessing from the Lord. They bring me joy even in distress.

Adam was released from the hospital two days later. I brought him home, and he slept with James and me for about a week. Adam only lasted a week before getting sick again. I had to take him back to the emergency room, and he was admitted again. I brought the children with me. They knew where the special room for children was located.

I would run back and forth between Adam and our other children. The staff were so good to my children and me. The doctor promised me that he would have a phone installed in our home in case of an emergency. After the visiting hours were over, I would say good night to Adam and pick up our other children. The next day I would come back to see Adam again.

Adam was such a lovable child that it seemed as if he had a magnetic attraction people were easily drawn to. He had really made himself at home at the hospital. On one visit to the hospital, Adam played with the lotion bottle. He had lotion all over his body including his head, feet, and on his clothes. He was also sitting on an apple. I asked, "Why are you sitting on an apple?"

"I'm going to eat it later, Mommy."

Adam was not only lovable but also very funny. He had a unique way of capturing a person's heart. Adam shared a hospital room with four other boys. One day, a man was visiting his son and said to Adam, "I guess you don't know how to talk. What is your name?" Adam paused for a moment. "You want to know my name. My named is Sammy Davis Jr."

The man smiled, and we both laughed. One of Adam's doctors was a Chinese lady who loved Adam, and he would run to sit on her lap.

On another visit, I came in and found out that Adam had been bad. Adam would run and hide when it was time for him to take his medicine, so the nurses put a net over the top of his bed, restricting his freedom. When I came in the room, Adam said, "Mommy, why do I have a cover over my bed?"

"It's because you have been bad."

I came to the hospital on another visit in which Adam's fever was so high that the doctors had him packed on ice. The doctors had been giving him shots apparently for pain. I was told to leave the room once to keep me from hearing Adam scream from the shots.

After so many long and tiring days at the hospital, I would go home and face James. In all the many days that I pressed through emotional pain, stress, and physical fatigue, James would not even offer to relieve me of some of the pressure. Out of all of Adam's hospital stays, James only made one trip to the hospital to visit his son. He never offered to go with me or to take Adam to the hospital for me when he got sick. I would get up during the night to check on the children, especially Adam, because of his illness. With all that I had on my plate, I almost always felt sleep deprived.

It was July 26, 1966, a few days after Adam was admitted to the hospital, and I had not slept for days. There was a knock on the door. It was the police with a telegram from the hospital informing me that Adam's condition was worse and to come quickly. I ran to ask Mrs. Holmes to watch the children because Adam's condition had worsened.

In the hospital, as I sat waiting for the doctor, it seemed like it was taking him a long time to come out. So many thoughts were running through my mind, and none of them were good. The longer I had to wait, the worse my thoughts became. After about thirty minutes, the doctor came out, and I asked him, "Is he any better?"

"Yes, he's not suffering anymore."

"Is he gone?"

"Yes, he's gone. Do you want me to send someone to help you?"

"No."

Hearing the doctor say that Adam was gone was more painful than anything that I ever experienced. I felt like my life was just knocked out of me. The tears started to flow. I called Dad and Mom and told them Adam was gone. I left the hospital to catch a bus home. After about two blocks, I got off the bus and walked the rest of the way home. I cried so hard that it was hard to distinguish between the rain and my tears. I walked in the pouring rain, drowning in my sorrow. Everything around me seemed to vanish. I felt all alone, dying from within. My heart was pounding in grief. It was as if time had stopped, and I'm stuck in this place of pain. My worse fear of Adam had come to pass.

Leukemia had overtaken him, and there was nothing I could do to save him.

After I arrived home, I broke the news to James and the children. The entire household was full of tears. Mom and Dad and Uncle Thomas and Aunt Estelle came over and spent a long time with us that night. Daddy took responsibility for all the funeral expenses. He made the arrangements with the undertaker. Everyone was very supportive. Family and friends offered to help relieve us of some of the smaller details for the funeral. Mrs. Hacker, one of Mom and Dad's dearest friends, bought Angela a dress to wear to the funeral and new outfits for the girls. We were only taking the twins, Angela, and James Jr. to the funeral. The rest of the children would stay home because they were too young to understand.

The funeral was very sad. Adam was dressed in a cute outfit, and a cap was placed on his head. James Jr. looked at Adam's body and laughed. He did not understand death. When we came to the burial site, I could see that Adam was the sixth child to be buried in the same grave site. I will never forget seeing those little coffins stacked on top of each other. At the repast, Daddy asked me, "Why are you not crying?"

"I have cried so much that no more tears will come out."

The pain was still throbbing like an open wound that would not heal. I had never experienced that kind of pain before. I did not know what I was supposed to do. All I knew was that my baby was gone, and I would like to keep every good memory of him with me. Adam had a head full of hair. I kept some of his hair in a plastic bag and one of his sweaters with me for a long time in memory of him.

Adam's death was very hard on the entire household. It was difficult for the children to understand why Adam was no longer with us. The twins were nine years old, Angela was six, and James Jr. was four years old at this time. Juliet and Jennifer were too young to understand to even discuss Adam's passing with them. The twins were the oldest, but they had difficulties in trying to understand Adam's illness and his untimely death.

Everyone, in some way, went through normal feelings of shock and disbelief. It appeared that his death affected James harder than it affected me. I made a huge effort to keep myself busy by engaging in daily activities with our children. This helped me to redirect my focus on doing something productive. I shared in the pain and grief of losing a child at such a young age as James did. The emotional pain and sadness ran deep inside of me. I am still in the state of shock that he is really gone. It is extremely hard for me to go to his room, knowing that I will never be able to tuck him into bed or kiss him good night again.

Sometimes when I'm picking up the children's belongings from the floor and I come across something that belongs to Adam, I feel just like a person touching a hot stove. The devastating pain and disbelief started to overwhelm me all over again.

I am glad that God has blessed me with children because looking at our children reminds me that I have something to live for. I always feel needed by my children. James was dealing with his grief in a very different manner. He did not reach out to me for comfort or to talk about it. For a time, James stopped drinking as much. He went from drinking every day to about twice a week. There was a noticeable difference in James's behavior when he did not drink much. His attitude was better, and his conversations made more sense. During his abuse of alcohol, his mood swings were erratic and violent, and he could not make a complete thought. Much of what came out of his mouth was nonsense. One example, when drinking excessively James would speak very badly about his coworkers. I noticed that when he was completely sober, his statements about his coworkers were pleasant and not degrading. When drinking, James would always blame alcohol for his actions. It was very rare that James ever accepted responsibility for his actions. The few occasions that he had were when he was without a drink for some time.

At one point, shortly after Adam's death, James started conversing about how his behavior affected his family. He said, "When I drank, I did foolish things, and I was destroying my family. I can't remember things that I've done when I was drinking. I treated you very badly. I love my family. I want to change. I am going to stop drinking."

I saw a different side of James after that conversation. I did not see James take another drink during this time. There were major changes in James's behavior when he was not drinking. He would spend quality time with the boys. He took them with him to Aunt Flo's house rather than leaving them behind. The children were happy to spend quality time with their father. James also helped around the house more. For example, when I washed clothes, he would fold them up. When I cooked food, James would wash the dishes. He was a completely different person at this point. James never told me directly what caused him to want to stop drinking, but I sensed that Adam's death may have spawned the notion to quit.

We all enjoyed the benefits stemming from James's soberness. The overall violence seemed to have gone down tremendously. We did not have to worry about him drifting into erratic mood swings or bursts of anger. There was more ease and less tension in the house. This dry time was a time of hope for all of us. For about a nine-month period, life in our house was the only time that we all felt a sense of normalcy.

On January 3, 1967, I started having labor pains. The pain became more intense, so James took me to the hospital. When I arrived at the hospital, the doctor wanted to send me back home, but I did not want to go back home. The doctor told me if I walk down the long halls in the hospital, he will see what happens. I kept walking as instructed, and four hours later, I delivered a five-pound, six ounces baby boy. We named our fifth son Milton. James was happy with the birth of his new son. I believe that Milton's birth helped ease some of the pain from the loss of Adam. The excitement and pampering lasted a few months. I had given birth to our eighth child. Who would have ever guessed that an only child like me would give birth to so many children? Right after birth, I asked the doctor to check for any congenital birth effects. The doctor checked him completely and told me there were no health problems.

In June 1967, I received a letter saying that one of my cousins from Florida was in Delaware visiting her sister. She wanted to come to New York to look for a job. She was about eighteen or nineteen years old and had just graduated from high school a year prior.

My cousin, Pam, arrived as scheduled. She was young, very energetic, and a bit on the wild side. Pam asked me to take her to Harlem. I tried to explain to her that Harlem was not a pleasant place, especially for a young lady her age to frequent. At one time, Harlem was known as the Black Mecca.

Prior to the Great Depression, Harlem was a booming city full of wealthy and middle-class whites. After the Great Depression, an influx of blacks moved into the city. Harlem became the hot spot for black entertainers and literary artists. It was only a couple of years ago that 1964 Harlem riots broke out lasting about six days. This riot sparked after a black youth was killed by a white police lieutenant. Tension and unrest were still the call of the day in Harlem. The city was decaying rapidly, and few people were opting to travel in that direction.

I could understand why Pam would want to go to a place that she thought provided an enormous opportunity to become successful, but Harlem was dangerous. I had a very difficult time trying to make her understand the dangerous reality about this place. She kept insisting that I take her there, so I took her, and she experienced firsthand that I had been trying to steer her away from. Shortly after we arrived in Harlem, we ran into a problem with some guys. We had to run fast to get away from them. We did not go back to Harlem after this incident. My cousin Pam finally saw the light.

After a couple of weeks, Pam and James went to the liquor store to buy some alcohol. Today, I still don't know whose idea it was to buy alcohol, but I know for certain that this event sparked a turn in James's good behavior. The children and I noticed an immediate change in his ways. His conversations were different. Almost everything that came out of his mouth was nonsense. He was back to his old nasty ways again.

Mom came over one day, and James was speaking foolishly to her. Mom told him, "You're drunk! Go lie down and sleep it off."

Meanwhile, Pam had no idea that she had awakened the beast that had slept for about nine months. Pam had not slowed down since she arrived at our place. One day, she decided that she wanted to go out to a party with one of her friends from Florida. She got dressed and went to the party and came back looking like a tramp. Her clothes were in disarray. Our children also noticed and commented about the way she looked.

She got to see for herself some of James's erratic behavior that we've experienced for a long time. On one occasion, Pam went into the bathroom, and James followed behind her and closed the door.

As soon as I saw James, I went to him and asked,

"Why did you go into the bathroom with Pam and closed the door?"

"I wanted to tell her something."

"Why did you close the door? You know the bathroom is private.

Pam then said to me, "I didn't know that your husband was so crazy!"

In my mind I thought, *you are partly the reason he relapsed.* James started drinking again and my cousin's wild behavior was a bit too much for me and my children to deal with, I spoke with her sister. I told her all that had transpired since she had been with us. Pam's sister said, "You do not need her around your children. I will send some money for her to come back here with me to Delaware."

After receiving the money my cousin Pam left to go back to Delaware. James continued in his erratic behavior. One day, he went downstairs and said several crazy things to a neighbor. He told her that I had a boyfriend and was cheating on him. The neighbor told him, "How can your wife have a boyfriend with all those kids? You get back upstairs and tell her what you are telling me!"

My neighbor came to me and told me about the incident. She told me everything that James said to her. She told me that she did not want this type of nonsense to get in the way of our friendship.

James's fighting continued to the point that on one occasion, the neighbors heard the loud disturbance and called the police. The police came and quieted him down. James apologized to the police, but the landlord got whiff of the incident and prior incidents and told us that we had to move.

Once again, we were kicked out because of James's angry tirades in which he punched holes in the walls, destroyed property, and abused me and the children. The landlord was very upset about all the damage James had imposed onto his house.

CHAPTER 7

South Ozone Park

Thanks to James, we were forced to move out of our Brooklyn apartment, but thanks to God, we were provided with another place to stay. Our Heavenly Father never once left us to live in the streets. Each time that we were up against a wall, He came through for us. I am so grateful for His faithfulness to us. Mom had spoken to her good friend Mrs. Terry about our situation. Afterward, Mrs. Terry came to us and spoke about a house she and her husband owned in South Ozone Park.

Moving back to Queens County again was a happy moment for me. Just the thought of being back in Queens was exciting. Going back to Queens would place me closer to my parents. Mom and Dad could come visit us more often in South Ozone Park. I also thought that this move might change James's attitude about life. Before we moved, James's behavior appeared somewhat pleasant, and he made me feel that he cared about us. James had spoken about wanting to buy a house prior to moving. We were both happy moving into a nice-sized house with a large backyard. James had also mentioned that he wanted to go back to work.

This move meant that our rent would increase from $200 to $225 per month. That was the highest our rent had ever been, but we would still receive a subsidy for rent. We were given the option to buy the house. The landlord was kind enough to say that she would apply our rent payments toward a down payment on this house if we wanted to buy this house. This was a really good offer that was too good to refuse. Since getting married, we have been moving from one apartment to another. For me, buying a house was something I only dreamed of doing. Daddy also felt this was a good opportunity and encouraged us to buy this house.

Mrs. Terry suggested that she could have a rent with the "option to buy" contract drafted for us to sign. James said that sounded good to him. I was glad to see that he seemed excited about buying a house. Two weeks later, Mrs. Terry came back with her husband, Mr. Terry, with a contract for us to sign. Mr. Terry was a very tall and big man. He was gentle and kind, but his appearance seemed intimidating to James. He had been growing his entire life, and doctors were unable to stop his growth. Mr. Terry was nearly seven feet tall and still growing.

When the Terrys asked if we were ready to sign the contract, James changed his mind. He told them to give him a couple of months and maybe he would make up his mind. The Terrys were very gracious and kind and agreed to check back with us. I believe that once James saw Mr. Terry, he changed his mind.

We did not have the luxury of paying for movers and a large moving truck this time. Instead, James borrowed a friend's truck and asked some of his friends and family to help us move. It took us a few trips to completely move all our belongings, but we were able to finish in one day.

We moved into a two-bedroom, one-bathroom house, which had a basement and two floors. We turned the downstairs dining room area into a third bedroom. There were two bedrooms and a bathroom located upstairs. We assigned all the boys in one room and the girls in the other room. We arranged a set of bunk beds and a single bed and a crib in the boys' room. Since Milton was only 20 and eight months old, we kept the crib for him to sleep in. In the girls' room, we arranged a set of bunk beds and a single bed. We brought the same furniture with us from our last other apartment.

Our bathroom was located near the top of the stairs. This bathroom was beautiful and spacious with up-to-date bathroom fixtures. It was fully tiled from floor to ceiling with shades of powder-blue design. Finally, we were blessed with an enclosed modern bathtub with shower doors and built-in shower heads. The blue-colored single vanity included a ceramic sink with pop-up drains and P traps, and white cabinets with self-closing door hinges situated below the sink. It was nice to also have a medicine cabinet for placement of our medicine and small toiletries. Right outside the bathroom was a linen closet, which made storing our towels and sheets much easier. Located downstairs was the kitchen, the living room, and the bedroom, which was previously a dining room.

Upon entering the house at the front door, we would step into a small foyer area. There was a coat closet to the left of the foyer. The foyer led directly into our living room. The living room led into our bedroom area. James built a bookshelf to act as a divider and provide privacy between the living room and our makeshift bedroom.

Veering to the right of our bedroom was a set of stairs that led down to the basement. Our kitchen was located on the first floor near the back of the house. It was large enough to place the dining table and chairs. The walls were painted white throughout the kitchen. The floor was lined with beige-colored tiles. There were two small windows. One window was situated over the kitchen sink, and the other one was close to the back door. I dressed the windows with shades and beautiful lace curtains to add a touch of elegance. I was pleased with the modern kitchen appliances. The landlord had bought a new refrigerator and stove just prior to us moving in.

We could exit the kitchen from the back door to go to our backyard. When exiting the back door, we would step down onto the stoop. The stoop was large enough to place a couple of chairs that overlook the backyard. The large backyard area was enclosed with a metal fence for privacy and security. The fence had a locking mechanism, keeping the playing children safe within the boundaries of the yard area.

I was glad that we were able to complete our move without any problems or major adjustments. This house provided us with more living space than before. We did not have as many bedrooms, but overall living space was greater.

After all the furniture arrangements were complete, I needed to take care of enrolling the children in their new schools. The twins were eleven years old now and would be starting the sixth grade. Angela was eight years old and would be in the fourth grade. James was seven years old, and he'd be in the second grade. Juliet was four years old, starting kindergarten. Jennifer and Milton were still too young to start school. Angela, James Jr., and Juliet were all enrolled in Jamaica Public School 96. I enrolled the twins at Shimer Junior High School.

When Juliet started going to school, I had a very difficult time getting her into the classroom. One male teacher saw how difficult Juliet was acting in getting her to go to class, so he stepped in to help. Immediately, Juliet took the man's hand without any resistance and went to class. On a different day, Juliet's teacher was absent, so she put on another tantrum and refused to go into the classroom. One of the male teacher's aides came and grabbed Juliet's hand, and she walked right in the classroom without a fight. It appears Juliet did not care much for female teachers but would respond without hesitation with the male teachers.

Shimer Junior High School

I enrolled the twins in Shimer Junior High School to start school right after Labor Day. I did not realize that there was an ongoing teachers' strike, which started in May of the same year, 1968. Apparently, the community took control of the school board and dismissed several teachers and administrators. Almost all the dismissed teachers were white and Jewish. This event caused major chaos in the city. Tensions between blacks and Jews were escalated and liberals and labor unions were engaged in a bitter dispute. This teachers' strike of 1968 caused all the public schools in the city to be closed for a total of thirty-six days from May 1968 through November 1968. We moved to South Ozone Park in the fall of 1968, so we missed some of the initial cataclysm between the school board and the teachers' union.

The situation at the twins' school seemed to be much more serious than I was aware of. The twins came home often from Shimer Junior High School complaining about the horrible incidents that were taking place in school.

Both twins spoke about bomb threats almost daily. There were concerns about students' and teachers' safety. I'm sure much of this stemmed from the teachers' strike, but it appeared that no one was able to bring any type of order to the turmoil. The city was in disarray because of the strike, and fallout was openly displayed in the classrooms and hallways of the schools.

I was shocked by some incidents that occurred at Shimer Junior High in particular. Some incidents were brought to my attention much later. The younger twin, Kenneth, referred to Shimer Junior High as drug infested and claimed that some teachers were allegedly raped at this school. Almost all the classrooms were overcrowded.

Kevin's description of the classroom was a free-for-all paper basketball–throwing contest in which almost all the students practiced their pre-NBA shooting skills. This was where some students would hold up trash cans while other students would practice shooting paper balls into them. Students were in full control of the classrooms and hallways. Teaching and learning did not exist within the walls of this academic institution. This was the call of the day, all in the presence of their teachers. The behavior in classrooms with a substitute was escalated to a much higher level of chaos and disorder. I did not know much about this until much later, and I was speechless. This was not the environment that I had hoped for my children to learn.

Turning Over the Table

Our move to South Ozone Park was without complications, and our children were now enrolled in school. It appeared that all of us had adjusted to our new environment back in Jamaica. However, it was always difficult to fully understand James's state of mind. It was about a month after our move. We were all sitting at the dinner table. The kids were enjoying their food, and everyone looked happy. Out of nowhere, James got upset and turned the table over and sent all the children to bed without allowing them to finish their food. I did not realize at that moment that James was drunk.

Later, he accused me of seeing another man that I had never met before, and he slapped my face. I yelled at him so loud that the neighbors could hear me,

"If you hit me again, I will call the police!"

He finally stopped and eventually fell asleep. Afterward, I went into the kitchen and made sandwiches and Kool-Aid and took it upstairs to the children. I did not want them to go to bed hungry. All the children were crying. Angela said, "Why does Daddy keep hurting you?" The other children had tears in their eyes also. Kevin and Kenneth said, "Mommy, we love you. Why is Daddy is so mean to you and us?" I told them, "Pray to God. He will fix it and protect us." It was extremely hard for me to see our precious children crying and so afraid of their father. I continued to hope and pray that God would end this nightmare my children and I were stuck in. I continued to look for ways to ease their minds from the reality of what was really happening.

Ms. Reynolds

I cannot thank God enough for placing godly friends who cared a great deal for my children and me. God always guided me to friends who weren't afraid of going the extra mile for a friend in need. It wasn't long after we moved into our house in South Ozone Park that Mrs. Terry, our landlady, introduced me to one of our neighbors, Ms. Reynolds, who lived around the corner. She was a Head Start director in South Ozone Park. She was a very nice person and regularly stopped by to see me.

During some of our conversations, I made her aware of how James treated me and the children. After telling her about James's behavior, she started coming by the house each day to make sure that I was okay. She always walked with her very large German shepherd.

One morning, she stopped by the house to see how we were doing. She knocked on the door, and James went to the door to see who it was.

Ms. Reynolds asked, "Is your wife up yet?" "

Yes, she is, but she is busy."

"Can I speak to her?"

"You can come back later." Ms. Reynolds insisted, "I want to speak to her right now. It's very important!"

After Ms. Reynolds's strong persistence, James finally came to the kitchen and told me that Ms. Reynolds was out there and wanted to speak to me. I went to the front door. Ms. Reynolds told me, "I just wanted to know if you were okay."

"I'm fine." "If anything goes wrong, please let me know because I'm here for you."

She kept checking on me from this day forward. Sometimes Ms. Reynolds would stop by twice a day. She lived about three blocks away from the school. We became very good friends. I mentioned to her that I wanted to go back to work. I told her that I had been looking for a job, but it was kind of hard with children. Ms. Reynolds agreed and then said to me, "I can give you a job.

You can come by Head Start, and I will give you work."

I replied in excitement, "This will be great!"

I really enjoyed working there. I was able to help with the children, type envelopes, and perform other tasks assigned to me. Ms. Reynolds gave me an opportunity to get out of the house and improve my job skills. She was so good to me that she also gave James some work to do. She had James make radiator covers for school and for her home and paid him for his work.

After about three months, James told Ms. Reynolds that I could not work for her anymore. I was so disappointed because I really enjoyed working there. James did not verbalize this, but I know that he did not want me working outside of the home. He always tried to keep me from becoming too close to anyone. I did not see it then, but now as I reflect, the more that I worked, the more self-sufficient I would have become. The mere thought of me becoming self-sufficient posed a threat to James's overbearing hand of control over my life. He continued to impose his restraints on me. He did not want me outside of what he could fully control. However, I continued my friendship with Ms. Reynolds.

I refused to allow James to take away everything that God had blessed me with. Almost every Saturday, Head Start planned some kind of activity for the children to participate in. Head Start would charter a bus and allow parents and children to go into the city to watch a movie or go to Brooklyn and other nearby areas as field trips. My children and I always enjoyed the trips and activities. The children were very excited about going places. But too often we felt like we were all on lockdown, unable to associate with the outside world.

It was sad that James would not go with us or participate in any school activities or special events at the school. Often, James tried to keep us from going. I kept pressuring and insisting that the children and I should go. James never seemed interested in anything outside of the home except the liquor store.

Ms. Reynolds continued to stop by our house to make sure that the children and I were okay. Of course, James's true colors were bound to be exposed at some point. He could not continue to portray the perfect husband to people outside of our home forever. On one cold winter day, James hit me and gave me a black eye. Shortly after, there was a knock on the front door. I went to answer the door. It was Ms. Reynolds. Of course, James followed me to the door. He would almost always follow behind me when I answered the door. James did not trust anyone around me.

Ms. Reynolds saw that I had a black eye and said, "I see that you have a black eye.

Where did you get the black eye from?"

I pointed to James as I replied, "James gave it to me."

Immediately, Ms. Reynolds looked at James and asked,

"Did you do that?"

"It was an accident," James replied.

Ms. Reynolds did not believe him. "No! This is no accident. You see this dog here? If I ever see another bruise on her, I'm going to let this dog eat you up."

James answered, "You won't put that dog on me!"

"Don't dare me! You just don't know me."

James did not say another word. He knew that she meant what she said.

James Jr. Fights in School

The children had been in school for a few months when I started receiving calls from the school principal, informing me that James Jr. was in a fight. Each time, I would go to the principal's office to find out what happened. James Jr. was accused of starting fights at his school almost every day. I was shocked and somewhat disbelief. I listened to the principal tell me that my son James Jr. was not innocent in these fights. However, this behavior was very inconsistent with his behavior at home. James Jr. was a good boy. This did not make any sense to me. I was unable to figure out why James Jr. kept getting into fights at school. When I questioned my son, he told me that kids in school were picking on him, but I was still left confused about the whole situation.

Well, it wasn't until James Jr. was around twenty years old when he told me the entire story. James Jr. told me that there was a bully at the school who was picking on him. James Sr. was constantly telling James Jr.,

"You need to fight for yourself. Don't let them beat you up. Be a man."

James Sr. wrote very offensive notes and gave it to James Jr. and told him to read it to the boys at school. James Jr. was afraid of his father, and he did not completely understand what his father had written. He read the notes to the boys at school as instructed by his father, and this started the fights. Each time James Jr. read a note his father wrote, a fight broke out at school. James Jr. was so afraid of his father that he felt that if he did not read the notes, the beating from his dad at home would be worse than his punishment from school.

James Jr. also told me that he beat one kid, Robert, who was one of the bully's followers. Later, Robert and James Jr. became very good friends. I knew that there was something that I was not being told when this was taking place, but I couldn't get a straight answer from James. I am so disappointed in the way that James Sr. chose to handle this situation. I am even more upset because I looked like a fool in front of the principal. I had no idea that my husband was largely to blame for these fights.

Whose Lipstick Is James Wearing?

The summer was gone, and the cooler weather had arrived. The temperatures for October 1968 usually ranged anywhere from a low of thirty-six degrees to a high of seventy-eight degrees. The weather had changed, demonstrating a new season, but James still refused to change for the better.

He continued to deny that he had any problem. The only change that the children and I seemed to experience in our household was from bad to worse and from worse to destructive. James had accused me of going outside of our marriage so many times that I did not keep track anymore. I have never once even considered betraying our wedding vows.

It was interesting how James acted when I confronted him with reasonable cause James had come down with his manly itch again. His itch was the desire to go out with the boys again. When James started expressing his strong need to go out, I knew that he was going to the bar to drink. He had begun to go more frequently again. One day while I was gathering the laundry to wash, his dirty clothes painted a suspicious picture right before my eyes. I came across one of James's shirts with a woman's red lipstick all over it. I confronted James about the shirt by saying,

"I was going through the dirty clothes getting the laundry together, and I saw your shirt was full of red lipstick all over it."

Before I could even finish talking, James jumped in and said,

"Oh, I know what happened. I was dancing the other night with that girl, and she did that on purpose. She just put that lipstick on me. It doesn't mean anything."

Immediately, I responded,

"Yes, I know it means something because if you were dancing with her why would she dance so close that she has to put lipstick on your shirt? It wasn't just one place. It was all over your shirt."

He tried to make more excuses. James tried to convince me that it was nothing to it. I looked at James and said,

"You have accused me of having boyfriends that I don't even know about, but I have never come home with any evidence for you to accuse me of."

Again, James interrupted saying,

"You need to just leave that alone!"

I came right back at him by saying,

"No, I will not leave this alone because of the way you talk to me and treat me. No, that's why you have accused me because you have someone else out there. You are always throwing stuff up in my face, and then you want to fight. You don't act like a man. You act like an idiot!"

"Let's drop it."

"No, I am not going to drop it. When you get on my case, you want to fight. I'm not fighting, but this is bad. This gives me proof that you do have someone else besides me. You never had any proof or reason to believe that I was cheating because I did not have anybody. I did not bring any type of evidence because I had nothing to bring home."

This conversation ended at this point, but I think he was ashamed, and he knew that I was telling the truth. The next few days, his behavior was a bit calmer. James went out and bought a box of chocolates and gave it to me. I guess the chocolate was supposed to make everything better. I let him think that I did not want it. When he presented the chocolate to me, I said,

"Oh, you are trying to bribe me."

I felt that he wanted me to keep my mouth shut. After that day, I left it alone. He did not talk about it anymore either.

I remember there was one occasion that Angela told me that she saw her dad talking to another lady. She said that she did not know who she was, but something did not seem right about it. Angela also said that he would go to make phone calls to someone and would talk in a very low voice. I wonder if any of this was connected to the lipstick on his shirt. But I did not have to worry about this. If James was cheating, it would not remain hidden forever.

Knives in the Basement

My life with James continued to turn in the wrong direction. Each time that I thought James's behavior was changing for the better, he would take several steps backward. It was around December 1968 to early January 1969 when I discovered something horrible that James was doing with the boys. James was taking the twins and James Jr. down into the basement and telling them to hold their hands out while he threw knives at them. He made the boys promise not to tell me what he was doing. One day, I went down to the basement and caught James in the act. He looked like he was shocked to see me come downstairs. I could not believe what I was seeing. In my anger, I yelled,

"*What are you doing?*"

"I'm making a man out the boys," James answered.

"You should never put their lives in danger. If I catch you doing this again, I will call the police!"

After this incident, I kept a very close eye on James and the boys. This was the last time that he ever did this. I was so shocked at what I saw. All I could think was that James could have seriously hurt our sons.

I found out later that this had been going on for some time without my knowledge. James was getting worse. I need God's hand of protection over my children and me. I was trying hard to protect them, but James continued to bring fear and pain to our lives.

What Are James's Trigger Points?

It was always difficult to figure out what would trigger James's next violent episode. Sometimes James and the children would be having a good time, and then he would suddenly snap into an angry rage. There had been times that James erupted because of a whisper, a stare, laughter, the rolling of the eyes, a raised voice, and too much fun, to name a few things. There was no real conversation pattern.

We were all trying very hard to figure out James's trigger point so that we could avoid it. This was nearly impossible because most often, there were no identifiable warning signs. A trigger could stem from the most unlikely of things, such as James's happy mood or complete silence in the house. In either case, James's mood swings whereas quick as darkness appears when someone turns off the light. Unfortunately, there wasn't a switch that could turn James's behavior back.

We all tried very hard to avoid any confrontation by trying to appease him even if we did not agree. James liked to tell jokes about being a great baseball player. Kevin called his father's jokes braggadocios—meaning that he did not only blow his own horn, but he inflated his stories so much that no one in their right mind could ever believe him. James once told the children that he was such a great baseball player that when he pitches a ball, all they could see was smoke. If the children didn't pretend to be entertained by his story, they would get whacked.

Murder in the News

It was during the month of March 1969 when Daddy came by the house in the middle of the night. I was shocked to see him at that time of night. I invited him in and asked,

"Why are you out this late at night?"

"I came to check on you and the children. I was watching the news, and I saw where a man killed his wife and all seven of his children. So, I immediately thought about you. You have seven children, and I wanted to make sure that you and the children were oka"Wy."e are all right, Daddy," I replied. "Thanks for checking on us."

The Church Banquet

There was an upcoming banquet at the church that I wanted to attend. I decided to go with Mrs. Hacker, Mom and Dad's good friend, for a ride to and from the banquet. I was really looking forward to the banquet, so I went into town to buy a dress to wear. I found the most beautiful red dress at Alexander's Boutique. I was excited because I had something nice to look forward to. The night of the banquet came. I got dressed, and the Hackers came by and picked me up. I enjoyed my time spent at the banquet. I didn't know the last time that I was able to attend an event such this one.

After the banquet was over, the Hackers brought me back home. As soon as I walked in the door, James met me and ripped my dress completely off me right in front of our children. He said that my boyfriend brought me back home. He refused to listen to me when I told him that it was the Hackers. James called me all kinds of profane names with no regard to our children. After ripping my dress off in front of the children, he said,

"Look at your mother!"

"Children don't look at me!"

James was out of control. The children were stunned at what he did. They were frightened and did not know how to respond. I was humiliated in the worst possible way in front of our children. This incident was so humiliating and painful to me that I had blocked it out of my memory until recently this year. I was watching the movie *Madea's Family Reunion* with Blair Underwood as one of the main characters. Blair Underwood's character was very abusive to his fiancée, Lisa, in the movie. This scene caused me to remember the horrible act that James committed on me the night of the banquet.

A&P Gunman

I remember an incident that happened in June 1969 that I will never forget. Believe it or not, I was able to leave the house without the children and without having any hassle from James for once. I told James that I would be right back, and I did not give him a chance to ask a bunch of questions. There was an A&P grocery store a couple of blocks away from our house. The store location was very convenient and easy for me to walk with my folding shopping cart.

Upon entering the store, I saw a man with a gun pointed at the manager. I was afraid and a bit nervous. Before I could digest the reality of this situation, the gunman yelled at all the customers,

"Move to the back of the store!"

After we moved to the back of the store the gunman yelled,

"If anyone move, I will shoot all of you!"

I was standing next to a little lady who appeared very nervous and scared. I whispered to her,

"Let's pray!"

So, we prayed, and shortly afterward, the police announced over the intercom,

"The gunman has been captured. Everyone is free to go."

"Thank God for saving our lives," I uttered. I quickly ran all the way back home. When I arrived home, I realized that I had forgotten what I went to the store to buy. I told James what happened in the store, and he responded like he did not care at all. He accused me of hanging out with a boyfriend the entire time that I was gone. James showed no concern for my well-being. I could have been killed, and he responded by accusing me of spending time with another man.

Again, I found some time to be alone again, so I prayed to God. "Lord, I seriously need your help now." I just want to say to all the young ladies or anyone who is reading this book who feel there is no way out. Don't stop talking to God because He is really listening, and

He is working things out for you no matter what. It's only God who will work things out. It was only God who worked it out in my case.

After praying, I really started going to church more often and spent more time praying and talking to the Lord.

September 1969: Mother Visits Again

Looking back at my life, I realize that God was always with me. Not knowing what to do, I wondered, *how can I get out of this marriage?* Things were getting worse, not better. I didn't realize that God was working things out for me.

In the fall of 1969, my mother came back to New York to visit me again. The children were happy to see her. My mother tried to be nice to James and had forgiven him for the past. For the first three days, he was nice to her. After the fourth day, I could see his attitude changing. On Friday night, Mother cooked a nice dinner for the family. The children were sitting at the table laughing and enjoying the food. James walked into the kitchen; I could see from the expression on his face that he was not happy. He walked over to the table and turned the table over with all the food. He yelled at the kids,

"Go upstairs and go to bed!"

My mother was upset with him, and she said,

"Why did you turn the table over? The children were happy. Why did you spoil it for them?"

He turned around, looked at me with a fork in his hand, and stabbed me in my side in front of Mother and the children.

"A dog is treated better than you treat your family! If you ever hit my daughter or my grandchildren, you can pick out a funeral home of your choice!"

Mother spoke very strongly to James.

"You have dogged my child and my grandchildren. They don't deserve this!"

James looked at Mother.

"I'm not dogging anybody." He didn't say too much after this.

After yelling at James, Mother came over to look at my stab wound. She and I were both grateful that the fork did not penetrate as deeply as we thought. James thought he had inflicted severe injury to my side. We did not tell him that it was not as severe as first thought. Mother started to clean and treat my wound. She told me what to do so that it will heal. I continued treating the stab wound as instructed, and over time, it healed without any complications.

Mother and I had a serious talk about my situation.

She said, "You do not have to live like this. You can always come home to Florida and live with me. You don't have to worry about clothes or money. You have family, and we will take care of you. You can wear my clothes, and Thelma and Dot's children are the same age as your children. Your children can wear their clothes. I was seriously listening to Mother. I kept praying to the Lord and listening to His voice.

A couple of days later, Mother packed her things to go back to Florida. The twins and I took Mother on a city bus to the subway to Pennsylvania Station to catch her train. After we saw the departure time for her train, Mother said,

"You go home. Don't wait because sometimes these trains are late. I'm okay. You go back because I don't want James to bother you."

The twins and I said our good-byes to Mother, and then we left to go back home. We made one stop along the way because Kevin wanted some pizza. We used the money that Mother gave us pizza and sodas. The twins and I enjoyed our moment together. It was rare for us to sit at a table without fear that our table would be overturned. We had to spend our money, or James would have taken it to buy alcohol.

Angela Calls the Police

Approximately one month after Mother left, James started acting nice again. He started taking the boys for walks. But not long after this, as we were eating supper, James yelled at me,

"I want to talk to you!"

"I'm talking to the children," I answered.

James came over, and again he turned the table over. I yelled at him,

"Enough is enough! I'm leaving you!"

I told the children to go outside.

"Mommy is leaving your Daddy."

I didn't know that Angela ran to a pay phone and called the police. I don't know where Angela got the money from. The pay phone cost ten cents. When the police arrived, James asked,

"Who called the police?"

Angela cried out, "I did."

She turned to the police and said, "My daddy keeps fighting my mother." The police claimed that there was nothing that they could do because it was "domestic." The police said that I could file a complaint against James, but I knew this would lead nowhere because abused spouses had no protection under the law.

The Little Black Book

After the police left, James went over to the chest of drawers and then pulled out his little black book. He acted as if this was his "get out of jail free" card or something that would prove that he was right. The book was his Union book. James would pull out this book many times during arguments and use it as his authority. For a person who did not know what the black book was, he or she would think it was his Bible.

Again, I thought our lives were getting better, but it was only getting worse. I was truly trusting God. I was learning to listen to His voice. The voice of the Lord was telling me,

"Believe and trust me. I will help you."

I was being obedient to God. I was reading His word more often, praying and trusting him. Now I know God was always and is still with me. I thank God that I never carried the thought of killing him. I did not want James to kill me or me to kill James or my children to kill him. Now that I am trusting in the Lord, I can see things in a better light.

January 1970: Backyard Events

It was 1970, and the New Year has just rolled in, and for a moment, our lives looked like they were beginning to get better. Sometimes we would all go into the backyard and play. James and I would jump in and play ball with the children at times. While we were all enjoying our time outside, suddenly something would trigger James. Someone may pass by or maybe speak to all of us. If it was a man who passed by and spoke to all of us, James would say he is speaking to me only. James's personality would change so abruptly because he thinks the man was coming after me.

Recurring Events

There were so many unbelievably cruel acts of abuse that my children and I suffered that it would take too long to pen each one each time the event occurred. Many of the abusive acts were recurring events. The abuse was often unpredictable and erratic with no real remedy for prevention found.

There was nothing normal about James's violent episodes. James's behavior often appeared consistent with a mental disorder such as paranoia, severe alcohol addiction, and Dr. Jekyll and Mr. Hyde syndrome. It's sad that all of these recurring events became almost a norm in our household.

The Dinner Table Experience

The dinner table experience became all too common in our house. In most households, the dinner table was a place to relax, enjoy a good meal, and communicate about the affairs of the day. Our dinner table experience would typically start out with everyone laughing and having a good time.

For some reason, James could not handle anyone laughing at the table. We did not know if James thought someone was laughing at him, but laughter seemed to trigger James's violent side. There were other triggers that would have caused James to erupt violently without warning at the dinner table.

Other triggers included but were not limited to having fun, smiling, making eye contact with him, silence, and talking. In each violent episode, James would turn over the table of food and command all the children to go upstairs and go to bed.

Time to Eat Knockwurst

This was another recurring situation the boys had to deal with. Sometimes at night, when James was drinking, he would wake up the twins and James Jr. and send them across the street to the delicatessen to buy him some knockwursts for him to eat. James would eat a pound of knockwurst by himself without sharing any. I would yell at James, telling him that the boys need their sleep because they have to go to school in the morning. James would reply,

"They need to be a man. Sometimes they may have to get up in the middle of the night. You never know what may happen."

This was James's idea of training the boys.

Bald Heads

The twins did not enjoy the way their father cut their hair. James would shave all their hair off. In James's way of thinking, taking it all off would keep him from having to cut it again so often. It was obvious that James never considered how the twins felt or how the other kids at school would look at them. Kevin was very vocal in sharing his dislike of going to school with a bald head.

Kevin described walking onto the school grounds with a bald head as extremely embarrassing. Other kids would start laughing from a distance. Some kids would walk up to them and whack them across the back of their heads and run away. This was total humiliation to both twins. Shaved heads were also recurring embarrassment. Loving parents would not find ways to humiliate their children.

Running / Playing Upstairs

Another repeated episode was when James would hear the children's footsteps walking or running upstairs. James would sneak upstairs and yell at the children. He would spank any one of the children who moved. When the children heard his footsteps, they would drop down in their beds and play dead for fear of their father's beatings. Afterward, James would come back downstairs and start a fight with me. The children were sorely afraid of him and were afraid to do anything.

Hidden Bottles

I never understood why James felt he needed to hide his bottles of alcohol. The children and I were fully aware of his drinking. When James was under the influence of alcohol, his whole demeanor and attitude would dramatically change. His speech, his erratic mood swings, and his inability to distinguish between reality and fantasy would betray him. The children and I have found alcohol bottles in so many places throughout the house. I have confronted him numerous times, but he seems to ignore me. We found his alcohol bottles under the bathroom sink, under the bed, in the clothes closets, in the stereo, behind books on the bookshelves, in the toilet tank, and of all places, in the baby carriage.

The baby carriage was the most surprising place where I found bottles. One day I decided to clean out the baby carriage. I took the carriage down and pulled out the mattress. To my surprise, I saw quite a few liquor bottles stored there. After seeing this, I thought, *Lord, I have been carrying liquor bottles with me. Someone could have easily thought that I was drinking.* I took the bottles and threw them all in the garbage. I approached James and said,

"You got me carrying all these liquor bottles around, and I don't even drink. I washed the stroller out and found a bunch of alcohol bottles. Why did you put all these bottles in this stroller?"

James answered, "I just didn't want to go to the garbage. I put the bottles in the closest thing near me."

I just don't understand why he continued to hide his bottles when he knew that we knew that he drank.

Spankings

James would spank the children for any reason, and sometimes he would even spank them for no valid reason at all. James Jr. later told me about an incident. James Jr. said that his father ripped the cord from the fan in the basement and then put his face on the mattress. He put a pillow over his face and spanked James Jr. with the cord. James Jr. told me that he did not know why he got spankings.

This was not the only time that James spanked our children in this manner. Most of them said that he would put them across his lap, pull their pants down to their bare bottoms, place a pillow over their face, and spank them. The pillow was suffocating, the exposure of their naked bottoms was humiliating, and the spankings were worse than painful. My children discovered later that near all of them suffered from some form of claustrophobia stemming from being smothered by pillows by their father.

Enemas

Another disgusting act that James inflicted on our children was giving them enemas. I do not know why James thought that he should give our children enemas when it wasn't warranted. This is something that James did often. The children complained that their father would put them across his lap, pull their pants down, and fill them up with an enema. James was not gentle but forcefully rough when inserting the enema tube inside of the children. They often said that they felt like they were about to burst from inside, and he would laugh. The children did not understand why their father was doing this to them.

Our children did not know that James filled the red enema bag with dish detergent and water. When he didn't have any dish detergent, he would take a bar of soap. He would use the soap to make soapy water and fill the enema bag to insert inside of our children. I yelled at him numerous times to stop giving our children enemas. He always said that the children needed to be cleaned out. I told him repeatedly that our children do not need this. This was abusive treatment.

One day, Mom came by and saw James giving an enema to one of our children.

Immediately, she yelled at him,

"Why are you giving that kid an enema?"

"They need it."

Mom yelled, "Your children do not need an enema. That's cruel. If I catch you giving another enema, I am going to report you to the law."

The enemas were harmful, not beneficial. I fought with everything in me to stop James from committing foolish and abusive acts upon our children. Trying to make him understand that his enemas were cruel was the same as expecting him to stop drinking.

Laundry Incident

There were so many incidents in which James treated the children very badly. There were some incidents that I only knew a portion of what happened. Sometimes I found out the full story years after when my children were already adults. For example, James did not trust me to go across the street and wash clothes. On one occasion, he told Angela and James Jr. to go wash the clothes. Since the laundry mat was across the street, it was close enough to see what was going on. On this occasion, Angela and James Jr. got into a fight over who was going to put the quarters in the washing machine. Neither of them was aware that their father was watching them. James would sneak down over to the laundry mat and hide while watching them.

When Angela and James got home, James made both sit on the bed and butted their heads together as punishment. I did not know anything about this punishment. I only knew that he hid from them and watched them argue across the street. It was James Jr. who told me about the punishment many years later. I was shocked and hurt by the amount of abuse to my children that was hidden from me.

It's Raining Money at the Phone Booth

Angela and I had gone to the store and were on our way back home when we stopped by the phone booth to call Mother in Florida. While at the phone booth, handfuls of coins started pouring out of the phone. Angela and I tried to grab all the money. Angela had a bag, which she used to put the money in. Angela and I agreed not to tell her dad about the money. Believe it or not, James saw us grabbing the money nearly a block away.

As soon as we arrived home, James took the money from her. Angela was furious with her dad for taking her money. Later that night, she tried to figure out a way to get her money back. The next day, Angela asked her dad for her money, but he refused to give it to her. Angela begins to stomp her feet, and she asked him again for her portion of the money. She said her daddy was telling her lies. James told Angela that he would buy her something with the money. As an eight-year-old, this was not acceptable to her.

They both came to an agreement. Angela created a money list, and each day he was to give her money to go to the store. Angela recorded it on a piece of paper. Often, James would steal the money, but Angela refused to let him keep it. One time Angela got so angry at her dad that she yelled,

"Daddy, give me my money back!"

She stomped her feet until he gave it back to her. James got so tired of Angela's nagging and demanding him to give her money back that he looked at Angela and said,

"Girl, here is your money. Just leave me alone!"

Eventually he gave her the remaining portion of the money. She refused to take no for an answer.

Angela refused to let her dad win. Angela was the only child who knew how to effectively demand something from her dad and make him do something that he did not want to do. Of course, this type of behavior was always prompted by James's treatment to Angela that sparked her resentment towards him.

License Plate Tag Incident

Since parking was limited to where we lived, it was common for people to park in front of our door or across the street from us. On one occasion, someone parked across the street from us, and James told Kevin, Kenneth, and James Jr. to go outside and write down the license plate number and bring it to him. The boys had no idea why their dad wanted this information. I was not aware of James's request.

However, the boys knew that if they did not do what he commanded, someone would get whacked. The boys did as commanded and gave the license plate number to their dad. As a result, James accused me of another man. He said that the owner of the car was one of my boyfriends, and he started unleashing his anger on my body again. The boys were heartbroken because they did not know that I would get punished for a stranger's car.

Beer Anyone?

It was bad enough that James drank alcohol in excess, but his warped philosophy on alcohol prevention was unheard of. One day, I caught James trying to give Angela a drink. I asked,

"Why are you trying to give her a drink?"

"This way she won't drink when she gets older."

"Stop trying to make her drink alcohol. Giving her a drink to keep her from drinking when she gets older is the stupidest thing that I've ever heard of. I better not catch you trying to give our children alcohol again."

I found out after the fact that James had tried to give several of the children alcohol a number of times, but they refused to drink. The children said their father would laugh as he tried to make them drunk. I thank God that my children were strong enough to resist their father's strong influence.

Pay Phone Incident

The children were very afraid of their father. At any time during the night, James would call from the bottom of the stairs,

"Psst, psst!"

The children knew that when they heard him make this sound, they had better come running. One rainy night, James called from the bottom of the stairs,

"Psst, psst!"

Although he was still sleepy, James Jr. got up to see what he wanted. James said,

"Come go with me."

Later, James Jr. told me,

"Daddy went to a phone booth to make a phone call. It was raining. I was standing next to him, and I moved a little, and Daddy punched a hole in my stomach with the end of his umbrella, and it started bleeding. After Daddy was done, we went back to the house. I was in pain, but I kept it to myself. I did not tell anyone."

This is another incident that was kept from me for years. James Jr. told me about this when he was an adult.

Manhood Training

For some reason, James assumed that his sons were not tough enough. He was constantly making foolish statements to the boys on what he felt they needed to become a real man. James's methods of training included handwritten offensive notes, baseball, drug checks, ice cream, and emergency drills, to name a few. I must warn you that none of his methods are found in any book and has not been endorsed by any human.

When James Jr. was faced with a bully at school, James would tell him, "Real men don't cry" and "Take it like a man."

To make matters worse, James wrote notes with very offensive language for his son to read to the bully at school. James's choices of words were not only profane, but it also provoked more hostility toward his son. As a result of reading the notes written by his dad, James Jr. found himself in one fight after another. Not knowing of James's involvement until years later, I was left to try to convince the principal that James Jr. was a good boy. James had a strong passion for baseball. He bragged often to his sons as he compared himself to the famous professional baseball player Bob Gibson. A talented pitcher who played seventeen seasons for the St. Louis Cardinals and won numerous prestigious awards including Cy Young Award, Most Valuable Player, and World Series champion and was inducted into the baseball Hall of Fame. I fail to see the comparison.

To prove his greatness to his sons and make his sons tough, James would take the boys to the backyard to play catch. James would throw baseballs at them as hard as he could and tell them to catch it with their bare hands. The twins were so afraid that they ducked, and James Jr. was wise enough to put on a glove. Even though James Jr. used a glove to catch his father's fastballs, he said his hand felt like his father nearly put a hole in the glove. All three of them were afraid to catch a ball from him. They were very small in stature. At the age of twelve years old the twins were probably around ninety pounds or so, and James Jr. was only eight years old and smaller in size.

Beyond their father's desire to prove his manliness by throwing a baseball as hard as he could at them, the twins actually liked baseball. Both of them enjoyed trading baseball cards with their friends at school. Trading baseball cards had become almost an art. The boys were always trying to acquire their favorite baseball card, but this required with to do so without losing their best cards. Kevin figured out that by leaving his favorite cards at home he could trade for other boys' top cards without losing his favorite cards.

Kevin developed a much stronger passion for the game of baseball than Kenneth. Kevin's love of the game remains intact even today. Kenneth enjoyed baseball, but his passion was aspiring to one day become a preacher. At a young age, Kenneth felt this was his life's calling but was not quite sure what to do with the call. If James devoted more time fathering his children rather than abusing them, he too could have sensed the call and helped nurture Kenneth in the development process.

Since the twins were getting older, James thought they should have girlfriends. The twins were not interested in girls yet, but James insisted. James asked the twins,

"Do you like girls?"

The twins replied, "No, sir."

James told the twins they should have a girlfriend, so he gave them money to buy ice cream sandwiches to get a girlfriend. When the twins came home, they pretended to have bought ice cream sandwiches for girls. The twins were clueless to how this would make them a real man, but they were too afraid to ask such a question.

The next method of manhood training James taught the kids was called emergency drills. In this method, the boys would have to be prepared to take their emergency positions with little warning. James would call an emergency drill when the boys were playing in the backyard. They were to run into the house as if there was a thunderstorm, go to their stations (separate corners), and sit quietly without any talking or whispering. The twins were kept separated because James feared that together they may start planning or colluding. If James heard talking or whispering, someone would get whacked. To this day, no one has figured out the objectives of this manhood training method.

Unfortunately, James's version of manhood training did not stop here. He continued to scare me and our children with his inexcusable actions. On the last Saturday in August 1970, we were all in the backyard playing and having a good time, and James went and picked up Milton, our youngest child. He started throwing him up in the air. I told him, "Stop throwing him in the air. You might drop him."

Right after I said that James dropped Milton onto the ground. It was a hard drop on the dirt. My heart started racing in fear that my baby was severely hurt. James picked Milton up and I ran over to grab Milton from James and to make sure that he was okay. His teeth were knocked out of his mouth. Milton was crying and I was so mad at James.

"Look at what you have done! I told you not to throw him up."

James looked at Milton and said, "I'm sorry, Milton, but this will make you become a man."

Milton was only three years old. It was a miracle that Milton did not suffer any injuries other than losing his teeth, thanks to God. Shortly after dropping Milton, James took Milton in the house to try to console him. He started playing with him, until Milton started laughing. Minutes later James took Milton to the store and bought him some ice cream.

Milton ate his ice cream and eventually started laughing.

Another method of manhood training was for James to check the twins' pockets for drugs. I guess you can call this periodic drug testing. I probably wouldn't frown on this idea if warranted, but Kevin said something that made sense:

"How can Dad check us for drugs when his breath reeks with alcohol?"

I wonder if James ever considered how his behavior has affected his wife and children. In all his questionable efforts and methods to prepare the boys for manhood, the boys have only one takeaway- fear.

As a father, James failed to give his children a pat on the back or thumbs-up as a form of praise or acknowledgment. His children never once received a hug from their father as a sign of his love for them. James's directives were never understood. Often, James spoke to the children with a very low voice like that of a whisper. Because he could not be heard, the children did not know what he expected of them. James did not offer to participate in any of the children's activities outside of the home. With all the negative enforcements from James, how could our children see their father in a positive light?

James Picks Up a Knife

It was a Sunday night in the latter part of June or early part of July 1970 when James started another fight. I do not know what triggered James; however, I do remember that he was drunk. James was a huge fan of the rhythm and blues singer James Brown and the singing group the Temptations.

It was very common for James to play his favorite songs on the record player repeatedly. On this night, James was playing his favorite music. He seemed to be enjoying the moment when suddenly, James got mad and started throwing things. He threw one of his records and a beer bottle. I yelled,

"You better stop throwing things. You may hurt someone."

Thank God James did not break the window or hit someone. It seemed that he wasn't paying any attention to me. The more I talked to him, the more violent he became, so I stopped talking.

Within moments, I saw James grab one of our largest long-handled kitchen chef's knives and started swinging the knife toward us. We were all scared and screaming in fear. James then started walking toward the front door.

When James turned the other way, I looked at our children and said,

"Let's get out of here!"

We ran out the back door from the kitchen to the side of the house near our bedroom window. I do not believe James realized that we were no longer in the house. We waited outside until it started getting quiet. After approximately thirty minutes, I heard the knife hit the floor. I peeked through the window, and I saw that James had fallen asleep on our bed, and the knife was on the floor. Before going back into the house, I said, "From now on do not put your pajamas on when you go to bed. Sleep with your street clothes on. You never know when we may have to run. I see that your father is asleep. Let's go in since he's asleep. You can go to bed, but do not make any noise. Be very quiet."

As soon as we came back into the house, I picked the knife up off the floor and threw it away in the outside garbage can. The children walked by tippy toeing into the house. They were very quiet and careful not to wake their father. I laid down on the couch in the living room. I was not about to go lie down next to James in our bed. It took me a long time to fall asleep. I was still very scared.

James did not wake up until the next morning.

After James woke up, he went upstairs to take a shower and rinse his mouth with mouthwash. When he finished, I confronted him.

"You need to stop drinking. You are getting worse. You are like a crazy man when you are drunk."

"What did I do?"

Immediately, I answered, "You don't remember?"

"I don't remember."

"You held a knife at us, and you were swinging it and coming towards us at the same time. We were afraid that you were going to hurt us."

James replied, "Oh, I didn't know that I had a knife."

I said firmly, "You are getting worse. You can kill us. I don't know how much more of this I can take."

"I'm sorry."

His apology did not sound or feel genuine. In my heart, I knew that each day was becoming more and more dangerous. Our lives are seriously at risk. The next three days went by without incident. By the fourth day, James got drunk and started fighting us again. I could never understand why James wanted to fight so much. At this time, I did not realize that James had a serious problem, but as I look back on several incidents, I realize that all of James's behavior was not because of his alcohol abuse. I have come to believe that James also had a mental disorder.

Are They Talking about Me?

I am reminded of another incident when James mixed wine and beer together to drink. His conversation started out nicely, and then his voice started to change. James heard someone talking outside. He swore they were talking about him. I tried to make James see that he was not making any sense.

"Those people are not talking about you."

James replied, "Yes they are."

"They are talking to each other. They are strangers."

"Do you know them?"

"No, I don't know them," I answered.

"How do you know that they are not talking about me? You are in with them. That's what's going on. They are covering it up for you. That's your boyfriend."

Once again, I am accused of having a boyfriend with people that I do not know. Go figure.

I began to wonder if we would ever see daylight. Living with James has felt like living in darkness with a raging bull. His unpredictability made it extremely difficult for me to protect our children and me at times. We were in constant fear and were terrorized almost daily by James's violent rage.

Fight at the Dinner Table

During the last week of August 1970, we were sitting at the table eating when James asked me a question. I do not remember his question at this moment, but I clearly remember that I answered him.

James looked at me and said,

"Didn't you hear me talking to you?"

"I answered you."

James got up and hit me, and then Kevin, Kenneth, and James Jr. came toward me to defend me. James grabbed Kevin and Kenneth and started punching them as if they were grown men.

I looked at James and yelled, "Leave them alone!"

"They need to stay out of grown folks' business!"

The boys ran upstairs to get away from their father. After the boys left, I looked at James and yelled,

"These boys are children and not grown men! They were only trying to defend me. You should not be punching them."

This is another instance that James failed to see his sons as children rather than adults.

The blows that James inflicted on his sons should not be taken lightly. James was so physically strong that when he inflicted punishment with his bare hands, it felt like a heavyweight boxer's punishing body blows. His blows were so heavy that after James hit me or the children, we hit the floor. Trying to reason with him was too often a no-win situation. That day was no different.

Mid-August 1970—Tab/Beer Incident

As time passes, I feel that I am falling into a never-ending cycle of abuse. I feel exhausted from the lack of sleep and having to keep a sharp eye on James day and night. I get up during the night to check on the children. I cannot trust James at any time. There was another incident in which I was glad that the Holy Spirit prompted me to be watchful of James.

One day I saw James open one of my cans of Tab diet sodas and put rat poison in it and then set the can back in the refrigerator. He was not aware that I had seen him. I was shocked at what I saw. I thought to myself, *this man is crazy. He's trying to kill me. What am I to do? I can't trust him. What if he poisons our food? How can I get away from his madness? If I find a way to leave, he will only hunt me down and kill me and my children.* I did not say anything to him. I started to pray to God,

"Please, Father, protect me and my children. Please do not allow James to kill us. Protect our food and drinks. Keep us safe from James's evil ways. I do not know what to do. Please help me, Father."

A few hours passed and James went across the street and bought five or six quarts of beer. He didn't have enough money to buy the liquor that he normally drank. After he returned, he came into the kitchen where I was and placed all his beer in the refrigerator except one. He began to drink one beer and then went into the living room and turned on some music. As soon as I pulled the lever on the can to open and drink the soda, James came rushing into the kitchen and slapped the soda out of my hand to the floor. He yelled,

You should not drink those. These diet sodas are not good for you."

In my anger, I took all of his beer out of the refrigerator and poured it down the drain in the sink and then threw the empty bottles in the garbage can in the backyard. I yelled at him,

You put rat poison in my drink, didn't you?"

"Yes, I did. I was just playing a game to see if you would drink it."

What would you have done if I did not see you put it in there?"

I was playing a game."

"How do you know that I wouldn't have drunk this?"

James's response was not sincere, and I knew he was not to be trusted. James did not attempt to apologize. After this incident, I would test everything before eating, drinking, or allowing the children to eat or drink because I could not trust him. I began to think to myself, *my situation has gotten worse. How do can my children and I get away from this crazy man?*

The Prayer and the Dream

That Saturday night, I prayed to the Lord and asked Him for help. I was very sincere when I said to the Lord,

"Lord, I have been praying, and I know that you are probably tired of me bothering you, Lord. Lord, please will you show me what to do? Should I stay here to make my marriage work, or should I leave my husband and go to Florida with my mother?"

That night I had a dream in which I could only see my mother's face. When I woke up, I knew I had the answer.

Letter to Mother

I have a doctor's appointment on Monday morning. I took my two youngest children, Jennifer and Milton, with me because they were too young to go to school. On my way, I took out the piece of paper, an envelope, and a stamp that I brought with me. While standing at the bus stop waiting on the bus, I wrote a letter to my mother, telling her that I was ready to come home. I told her about the dream that I had and how the Lord showed me her face, so I knew that I was making the right decision. I promised to call her as soon as possible.

Dad Shows Up

I knew that she would not receive my letter right away, so I planned to call her. It was amazing to me how Daddy showed up at our apartment when he did. Daddy would come by sometimes and take them to his house and give them treats. It was Monday afternoon after I mailed the letter to Mother.

Daddy said to me, "I've come to pick up my grandchildren to take them to the house."

So, I said to Daddy, "I want to come too." I told James that I was going to my dad's house. I was glad that James didn't say a word.

When I arrived at my dad's house, I told Daddy and Mom what I wanted to do. I said, "When my mother came up last year, she told me that I could come home, and she would help pay for me to come home. She assured me that I would not have to worry about packing clothes. She told me that I could come with the clothes on my back if I had to." I looked at Daddy. "I want to leave."

Daddy responded, "Are you sure?"

"Yes, Daddy. I can't stay there anymore."

My dad listened to me. I went on to say, "When you come by, I'm going to pack a few clothes, but I want James to think that I'm giving these clothes to somebody. These are going to be my clothes." I didn't tell Daddy when I was really going. I told him, "I need to go. Can I call my mother?"

I called Mother, and Daddy spoke to her also.

Daddy told her, "By the time you get the money here, it will be late."

Mother said, "I'm going to have to borrow the money. I have a good friend who told me in case of emergency she would let me have some money. If you can get the money, give it to Theodosia, and I will send the money back to you."

At that point, I still had not told Daddy exactly when I was going to leave. I didn't know when I was going to leave, but I knew that I couldn't take it anymore.

Saturday Night, September 5, 1970— Iron Incident

The next Saturday night, I was ironing one of James Jr.'s white shirts because he was going to get baptized the next Sunday. While I was ironing the shirt, James came over and cut the ironing cord. I then looked around in the kitchen. I did not see anybody; none of my children were there. I took that iron and threw it at him, and it broke the kitchen window. I was angry, but I just missed hitting him.

James looked at me and yelled, "You crazy?

Why are you throwing that iron at me?"

I yelled back at him, "Why did you cut the cord? You saw me ironing this boy's shirt."

Thank God I was finished ironing James Jr.'s shirt. James did not know that I was finished, but he had no excuse for cutting the cord. I still did not know when I was going to leave to go to Florida. I only knew that we would not survive here much longer.

CHAPTER 8

The Exodus

Sunday Morning—September 6, 1970

When I got up Sunday morning, I felt pretty good. While I was in the kitchen cooking, a voice said to me,

"Why not leave today? This is your time."

I had begun to listen to God's voice more, and on this one morning, it seemed that God's voice was stronger, and He gave me strength. I felt like I was close to God. I decided that I was going to be obedient and listen. I started to pray.

"Lord, I have been through a lot, and I am tired. Enough is enough. Now, Lord, I sense that you are leading me on the way out, so why don't I take this way out. Lord, I want to go to Florida tonight after the baptism. Lord, will you help me to get there? Please make a way that I can get there."

After praying, I started to think about transportation to leave. I mumbled to myself, *"Daddy's car had been stolen. I'm not sure how we can leave."* So that morning, I decided to cook a big dinner for James. I knew that we were not going to be here to eat it. I cooked enough food to last him for a few days.

I kept James Jr., Juliet, Angela, Jennifer, and Milton home with me Sunday morning. I deliberately kept James Jr. at home with me so that I could take him to the six o'clock evening service. I knew that if James Jr. had gone to church that morning, James would have found a reason to stop me from going to the evening service that night. The twins went to Sunday school with my parents like most Sundays.

Before leaving home, I told James that I needed money for the bus fare. James replied,

"James Jr. could have gone to church this morning and got baptized." I said to myself, *I know that. That is why I kept him home with me. I knew that you would try to stop me. I'm getting ready to leave your butt.*

James gave me ten dollars and told me to bring his change back.

"Okay," I said. Then I kissed him on the cheek. We left home around 3:00 p.m. My five children and I caught the city bus to church from Ozone Park to the heart of Far Rockaway. Again, I prayed to the Lord. *Please do not let anything get in the way of us leaving today.* We arrived at church in time for the six o'clock evening service.

Six O'clock Evening Church Service

I was sitting in church with all my children except James Jr. because Daddy had James Jr. who was being baptized. Kenneth and Kevin were sitting close to me. I whispered to them, "Look, boys, we are going to Florida tonight."

Kevin said, "We are!" He was excited.

Kenneth had tears in his eyes and said, "No, Mommy, we can't go because Daddy will kill us."

"No, Daddy will not kill us. Daddy won't hurt us no more because we are leaving Daddy," I said.

Then I went up to where James Jr. was getting baptized. After James Jr. got baptized, I went downstairs where the men were helping

James Jr. change clothes. I gave James Jr. a hug and then went to my daddy and asked him for the money to go to Florida.

Daddy responded, "I don't have any money on me. It's in the bank. Tomorrow is Labor Day, and I can't get it until Tuesday."

"Daddy, I cannot go back home. I cannot go back!" I quickly responded.

I was so desperate that I was willing to stay at the train station if necessary. Then Uncle Thomas, Daddy's brother, came downstairs with a stack of money. I don't know if the money he had with him belonged to the church or if it was his own personal money.

Uncle Thomas asked Daddy, "How much do you want? Three hundred dollars, four hundred dollars?" I believe Daddy told him three hundred dollars. I knew that I did not have to pay for everybody. Uncle Thomas gave Daddy $350. He said, "I'm giving you fifty dollars that you do not have to pay back. This is for them to get food on the train." I thought this was a smart idea.

Before leaving the church, I went over to Mom to say good-bye to her because she had a function to attend at the church. She looked at me and said, "I hope that you do not come back. Do not let him sweet-talk you into coming back to him."

I responded, "Unless God comes down to earth and tells me to come back, then I will not come back."

We embraced in tears while my heart was deeply saddened; I knew I was doing the right thing. I will always keep Mom in my heart because she embraced me as her own daughter. After this, we left the church and went back home with Daddy, but I realized that Daddy was driving someone else's car. I don't know whose car it was. We packed a small lunch.

Next, Daddy called Mom's cousin John, a taxi driver.

Daddy asked, "John, can you take my daughter and her children to the city to catch a train to Florida?

"What time?" said John

"I believe there is a train that leaves out at ten o'clock tonight." "I will be there in about an hour."

When John arrived Daddy asked, "How much will you charge me to go to the city?" Daddy explained the situation to him.

The driver said,

"Because of this situation, I will only charge you twenty dollars. I normally charge fifty to sixty dollars to go to the city. Since you are my relative and you are doing it for a good cause, I will not charge you that much."

When we arrived at the train station, Daddy went over to buy our tickets. He did not have to purchase tickets for everyone. He only had to pay for me and the twins. I didn't think he had to pay for Angela, who was ten years old at that time. After the tickets were purchased, we were walking down the stairs, and Daddy was trying to give me the tickets. Just then, the train started moving slowly.

I yelled to the conductor,

"Conductor! Please stop the train! My children and I want to go to Florida."

The conductors pulled the emergency brakes and stopped the train and let us get on. I knew at that point that this was God's plan. His plan worked out. My plan failed. God's plan is always better.

The children were very happy on the train ride. We did not have to worry about anyone giving us the evil eye or yelling at us. My children were so wild on the train. The patter of their little feet was such a beautiful sound to me. Each time one of them ran by me, I could hear the sound of freedom that we longed for. This was the first time that they had experienced this type of freedom. Seeing my children so happy brought tears of joy to my eyes.

On the train, I met a woman who asked me, "Where are you going?"

I replied, "I'm going to Florida."

"Are you visiting?"

"No, I'm moving to Florida. I'm leaving my husband."

Afterward I started telling her some of the things that happened in my life.

Then the woman said,

"I went through a similar situation, but I ended up divorcing my husband. You are a brave woman traveling with all those children. How many children do you have?"

"I have seven children." I did not leave any of my children behind, and I have no regrets for my decision. If it wasn't for my children, I don't know what I would do. My children were my fighting piece. I would give up my life for my children.

We arrived in Jacksonville, Florida, the next day, which was Labor Day. The train ran a different route from the normal route. The normal route would have taken us all the way to Palatka. Jacksonville was our final stop. Mother and Papa Albert drove to Jacksonville to pick us up. When Mother saw me, we both started crying. It was hard to believe that I was back in Florida. My last visit to Florida was seven years ago.

I have now come full circle after twenty years. I left my mother in 1950 at the age of fourteen for a better education and life in New York. I never imagined that my life would have taken such drastic turns. Now at thirty-four years of age and seven children, I'm about to embark on a new phase of my life in the same place I left twenty years ago.

CHAPTER 9

A New Beginning

The last time I came to Florida to visit, I said that I never wanted to come back here to live. That was in 1963, seven years ago, when I came to visit Mother for two weeks. I did not want to face the old segregated system of living.

The South was still full of prejudice towards Blacks, and everything was still segregated.

I moved to New York in 1950 because my parents believed that I would receive a better education and have a better opportunity to become successful in life. I had become accustomed to the modern conveniences and freedoms available in New York that I never would have experienced in Florida.

In 1950, when I moved to New York, I left an old system of racism and segregation in Florida and throughout the South. This system of living glorified whites and degraded blacks as less than human beings and denied blacks of their constitutional rights.

Unfortunately, I was born into this demoralizing way of life and lived under its rule for the first fourteen years of my life. After I moved to New York, I learned and embraced the freedoms granted to every American citizen regardless of the color of their skin.

None of my children had ever experienced the prejudice that existed in the South. The Jim Crow laws of the state and local areas demanded separation of blacks from whites in all public places and facilities. These unconstitutional laws commanded service of a white person ahead of all blacks. Segregation was enforced across the spectrum in areas of public facilities, employment, transportation, medical care, education, and housing. I was reminded of the ills of the South almost immediately upon my arrival in Palatka.

Integration had begun in some public facilities. Some places were fully integrated while others were moving toward integration at a slower pace. However, there were certain places that remained fully segregated.

One of the public facilities that remained unchanged was the restaurants. Before I moved to New York, blacks were not allowed to sit in the same room as whites in a restaurant.

Blacks were seated in the back area of a restaurant. When ordering or picking up food, blacks would have to go to the back of the building. They were never allowed to walk through the front door of a public establishment.

When I came back to Palatka, Florida in 1970, restaurants were still operating in the same manner.

A few public facilities that had changed after I returned to Palatka included seating on the train, schools, and hospitals. Before I left for New York, blacks were only allowed to ride in the rear of the train on coach. When I returned, blacks could sit anywhere that they had purchased a reserved seat.

Before I left Florida there were all black schools and all white schools. The white schools received new desks, books and other school items. The black schools would only receive the used desks and used books from the white schools after the white schools received new items. When I returned to Palatka, the schools were fully integrated. All-white and all-black schools were a thing of the past. Before leaving for New York, the hospitals would place all white patients in one room and all black patients in a separate room. When I returned, the hospitals were fully integrated. Patients no longer had to be separated by the color of their skin.

Some of the public facilities that were beginning to change when I returned to Palatka were the hotels and the department stores. Before leaving for New York, the hotels maintained separate white sections and separate black sections. This had begun to change when I returned to Palatka. There were very few black hotels that blacks could frequent when traveling. When I left Florida blacks would have to wait in the back of a line in a retail department store for check out. If a black person was in line and a white person came up, the white person would go ahead of the black person even if the black person was in line long before the white person. However, there were some people who are courteous enough to let a black person go ahead of the white person if they were already in line.

I was reminded of the old system in the South shortly after my return when Mother and I went to buy some burgers for all of us to eat. When we arrived at the restaurant, Mother told me to go to the back and pay for the burgers.

I responded to Mother by saying, "I don't want to be disobedient, but I don't want to go to the back of the restaurant. Why don't we just buy some hamburger and cook it at home."

Mother agreed with me, so we did exactly that. Going to the back of the restaurant was one example of how blacks were treated as less than second-class citizens.

It wasn't long after moving back to Florida that I found myself gazing outside of my mother's kitchen window wishing that I was not there. I saw some things that had not changed since I was here the last time. I started to pray,

"Lord, please forgive me. You are the one who brought me here, so I need to make the best of it. I can't go back to New York, or I will be killed." After praying, I started to keep busy to take my mind off things. I cleaned my mother's house, and eventually those thoughts were gone.

For the first two months, we all were living in Mother and Papa Albert's two-bedroom house. It was a very tight condition. The house had two floors and a basement. There was only one bathroom, which was in the basement. The living room and the kitchen were located on the first floor. The two bedrooms were located upstairs on the second floor. For sleeping arrangements Mother and Papa Albert slept downstairs in the living room. The boys slept in one room upstairs, and the girls slept in the other room upstairs.

Making the adjustment to our new living situation was difficult. I did not know how we were going to make it. However, things started to fall in place right before my eyes. People started giving us many items that we needed. Someone gave me some folding beds for the children to sleep on. Mother allowed me to wear her clothes. Aunt Dot and Aunt Thelma, who were more like my two sisters, shared their children's clothes with my children.

I was able to get all the children enrolled in school without a problem. My children were able to walk to school. There were numerous adjustments that had to be made from living in a large city to living in a very small town. For my children, this transition was more of a culture shock. My children did not understand the language in the South, and people here did not understand my children's heavy New York accent.

In New York, we always had reliable transportation, modern conveniences, and many options for entertainment. On the other hand, Palatka lacked public transportation and entertainment was almost nonexistent. Since we did not own a car, we had to rely on transportation from Mother or Papa Albert when we were unable to find other means to travel in town. We became accustomed to walking to most of the places that we regularly frequented.

Unfortunately, we did not have the luxury of living within a block or two of retail stores, schools, or any church. However, we did not complain; we made the adjustments and placed one foot in front of the other as life moved on. We always made it to our destination with little or no problems. We were very grateful for all the help provided by Mother and Papa Albert and others, such as Thelma and Dot. Many of our family members donated numerous items and offered their time to help us in making such a huge transition.

When we arrived in Florida, we had no idea how we were going to survive, but I knew that God did not bring us out of physical and emotional bondage to say, "Okay, you are on your own now." We knew that we would be faced with challenges, and we did not expect a bed of roses. At times, we had to take things one day at a time. Often, we had to focus on one problem at a time.

Physically we were no longer in harm's way, but emotionally the abuse had taken its toll on each of us. Each one of us was terrified, and we feared that James was going to find us and kill us. I found myself jumping at even the smallest sounds such as when the phone rang or a knock on the door. My children and I found it hard to sleep at night. All of us experienced nightmares of James finding us.

My children were instructed to be careful and walk together with the neighborhood children. Precautions had to be taken for my children's protection and mine. Mother and Papa Albert did not allow us to answer the phone, just in case James called. James did not help matters because he started calling each day while we were at Mother's house. I found out from Daddy that James called Daddy the same night that we left New York.

He asked Daddy, "Is Theodosia and the children at your house?"

Daddy answered, "No."

"She said she was going to church."

"She was in church."

"Do you know where she went?"

"The last time that I saw her she was on her way home."

There was a brief pause, and then James declared, "If she is not home by morning, I'm going to have to get the FBI to look for her."

Mother told me that James also called her house looking for us. We arrived in Palatka on Monday afternoon, and James called that night. Papa Albert answered the phone.

James asked, "Have you heard from Theodosia and the children?" Papa Albert answered, "No."

"Are they with you?"

"No."

"You don't know where she's at?"

"That's your wife. You better find her, and she better not be hurt either!"

After this conversation, James called every night. He also called Daddy and Mom almost every night until they decided to change their phone number and made it unlisted.

We lived at Mother's house for nearly two months, and James continued to call every day while we were there. After we moved out, he also continued to call Mother and Papa Albert. One day James asked if he had heard from us, and he asked Papa Albert for our phone number. Papa Albert gave him the wrong phone number to get him off his back. James continued to call Mother and Papa Albert for years.

Mother told me that James would change his voice when he called and he would ask for the children by name as if no one knew his voice. Mother always recognized his voice and did not fall for his trap. I remained very fearful for a long time. I realized that my sanity was kept in check only by the grace of God. He did not allow this fear to completely take over my mind. Fear is something that can paralyze a person and prevent a person from being able to function normally in daily activities.

Living with James was paralyzing both physically and emotionally. The thought of James finding us ran through my mind often. At times it was hard for me to focus, especially when a stranger showed up without any warning. I remember how I became very nervous once after I had applied for public assistance. Back then when a person applied for public assistance someone would come to the home for an interview with the applicant before granting aid.

One day, a man came to our house, and he asked one of our neighbors where I lived. The neighbor told the man where I lived. I started to think that if James was here looking for me, my neighbors would tell him how to find me without asking any questions. I was beginning to think that I was not even safe here. I felt very shaky.

When the man came by to interview me, he showed me his identification badge and introduced himself. This gave me some relief because my nerves were getting worse. I went on to tell him, "I was afraid that my husband may have been sending someone out here to look for me." The man told me, "Don't worry, you will be all right.

Mom told me about a month after we left New York that James came over to their house. At this time, Mom and Dad had three foster children whom they had been caring for at their house. James asked my parents if he could stay in their basement. He offered to give my parents some of his food stamps to help them with the food.

Daddy looked at James and said, "You were not nice to my daughter. You were evil and mean, and you beat her up all the time. Why do you think I want you to come here and stay with us? No, you can't stay here."

Mom realized what James was trying to do, so Mom looked at Dad and said, "Honey, we need to go to the store. We need to pick up some stuff that the kids need for school." Mom did this so that the kids would not open their mouth and say something like Big Sister is down in Florida. My parents rushed them out of the house.

Every night, James would try to collect phone call. He knew that I called Mother through collect call, so he tried the same thing. Neither Mother nor Papa Albert would accept the charges for his phone calls. From this point on, I assumed that he must have found some money to call long distance.

A Place of Our Own

Our temporary arrangements were very tight at Mother's, but we were grateful for having a roof over our head without the daily terror that we experienced in New York. After two months back in Florida,

Uncle Phillip, who was first married to Papa Albert's sister Alberta, had a house he wanted to rent. This house was very close to Mother and Papa Albert's house. Mother had spoken with Uncle Phillip told her about my situation and asked if he would rent it to me. Uncle Phillip said he would rent it for eighty dollars per month. Mother told him that was too much because I did not have much money, and she and Papa Albert were going to help me. Uncle Phillip lowered the rent amount to forty dollars per month, and Mother felt this was acceptable.

Later, Aunt Juanita, Uncle Phillip's second wife, came over one day to tell me that they were planning to sell the house for three thousand dollars. She told me that she wanted to offer it to me first. I talked to Daddy and Mother. Daddy thought it was a good idea. He said the house was only worth the land that it was on. Daddy said he would send me five hundred for the down payment, and he would help me make the payments. Aunt Juanita paid for the attorney fees, and she promised to work with me. My monthly payment was seventy dollars per month, and I paid it off in nearly two years.

House Description

This house that we moved into was located very close to Mother's house. It was one street over in the same neighborhood. Our house was a very old two-bedroom house situated on a dirt road. There was a screened porch in the front of the house that was turned into a bedroom. This was the room that the three girls shared. Next to the girls' room was another bedroom that I occupied, and to the right of my room was a bedroom which the four boys shared. To the right of the boys' room was the bathroom.

The bedroom floors were lined in linoleum flooring, which was inexpensive and easy to clean. All the walls were made of sheetrock, but holes were found throughout the house. Because of the holes, we always felt that we shared the house with uninvited guests, such as mice, roaches, and sometimes snakes, which would try to enter.

Upon entering the front door of the house, we would walk into the living room area. The living room led directly into the dining room and then into the kitchen. The dining room area was large enough to place a dining room table and chairs for all of us to sit and eat. We sat at a small kitchen table and chairs in the kitchen. There was a back door in the kitchen that led to a back porch. There weren't any light fixtures on the back porch, leaving it very dark and creepy at night. The back door did not have a security lock on it, leaving us susceptible to burglary. I placed a chair up against this door to make it difficult for someone to break in.

The flooring in the living room and the dining room were lined with very old carpet. It was sometimes difficult to see the carpet because the dirt was matted from years of buildup. When we moved into the house, we did not have a vacuum cleaner, so we swept the carpet each day. It was hard to clean this house because everything appeared to be as old as the house itself. There wasn't much improvement when we cleaned it.

This house had some other issues such as a leaky roof, and it lacked central heat and air.

When it rained, we placed buckets throughout the house to catch the water. Daddy and Uncle Thomas came to visit us several times and worked on patching and fixing many structural problems in this house.

During their visits, Daddy and Uncle Thomas patched our roof, replaced sheetrock, painted the house, fixed plumbing and fixed nearly every problem they saw. The children and I enjoyed every moment of their visits.

During the warmer months, we placed box fans in the windows to cool the house down. Most of the time, the fans only brought in hot air from outside to mix with the hot air inside. We also used circulating fans throughout the house. During the colder months, we used portable kerosene heaters to warm the house. The disadvantage of using kerosene was that the smell was strong and unpleasant. The kerosene heaters weren't always enough to adequately heat the house; therefore, I would turn on the oven and leave the oven door open. For us living in this house was backwards because we had free air conditioning in the winter and free heat in the summer.

The location of the house made life a bit challenging because it was on a sandy dirt road. Many times, people were afraid to drive their cars in front of our house because their cars got stuck in the sand. There was a streetlight outside in front of our house, but it was quite dim. The streetlight was not bright enough to deter strangers from lurking around. We always felt uneasy because of how dark it was around our house at night.

Our yard was mostly dirt, weeds, and trees. We had very little grass around our house.

With the many trees that were so close to our house at night, it felt like our house was amid a jungle or a forest. At night, we could hear animals outside tearing into our garbage cans. The raccoons here were bigger than the average raccoon. Some of the raccoons looked more like a dog rather than a raccoon. At times, we found snakes, lizards, and stray cats and dogs, which all tried to make our house their home.

We did have some neighbors who lived on the same street and were very close to us in our neighborhood. Over the years, most of them died, and we were the only family living on our street. When this happened, the grass and weeds grew tall around the other houses making us feel as if we were in the center of a jungle or a forest. Regardless of all the structural problems of our house, we made it into a home by instilling the love of God from within us. We shared many special times together as a family.

We watched shows on our black-and-white television, and we enjoyed many shows including family shows, such as *Little House on the Prairie*, *The Waltons*, cartoons, *Sesame Street*, and of course sports, to name a few. We found a way to enjoy each other's presence.

As a family, we were not exempt from the growing pains of life. My children experienced bouts of disagreements among each other; tempers flared, and feelings were sometimes hurt. One of our most challenging foes was not each other or other people, but the financial struggles from being poor.

There were numerous times that I did not know where the next meal would come from. I can also remember occasions on which my children needed shoes, clothes, money, or items for school when I did not have any money. There were so many times that I had more bills than I had money. In each of these times, God made provision for all our needs. We did not own the latest brand names or fashions or the hottest item for sale; nevertheless, we had peace in knowing that all our needs were met. We were grateful for the smallest of blessings and learned to appreciate everything from God because there were so many people who did not have what we had.

We had so many reasons to thank God for our lives each day; we were free from the bondage that enslaved us for such a long time. I believe that God allowed us to face these challenges so that we would not forget that it was He who delivered us and that He is our source. When we prayed, our Heavenly Father answered. Despite the bumps in the road, we always landed on our feet exactly where God planted us.

As I look back over our times together as a family, there is one constant that was always present in our home. This one constant was that we prayed together as a family. Many nights, the children and I gathered around my bed. There was never a dull moment in our home, but our times together were always sealed in prayer.

There were many days of laughter in our household; most were spearheaded by James Jr. He had a way of making us either laugh or cry. He found a way to make us laugh from his pranks or cry from the fear ignited by his pranks.

Search for a Job

I truly enjoyed our time together; however, I needed a job to pay the bills. I decided to look for a job. I looked through the newspaper for job openings. I saw a secretary job at the courthouse. I walked to the courthouse and was told they had just hired someone. I also saw a teacher's assistant position available at the school. I had to take a typing test and was happy that I passed the test. Human Resources told me that I would have to wait to find out if I would get hired.

In the meantime, Mother introduced me to some people who wanted someone to clean their houses. I was paid ten dollars a day for each house that I cleaned. I had quite a few houses that I cleaned. People liked my work, and I was recommended to others to work for. After cleaning houses for a little short period, Aunt Thelma, who worked at the hospital, told me about a position available at the hospital. I applied for this position and was called in for an interview. I was scared and nervous during the interview. I was sure to pray before I went in.

During the interview, the supervisor asked me several questions to see if I had the skills to do the job. However, some of his questions were related to the care of my children.

The supervisor asked, "How many children do you have?"

"I have seven children."

"How can you work with all those children? Who will watch your children while you work?"

"My mother watches my children for me."

"I see you have things covered. I will get back with you in a couple of days."

The next day, the administrator called me and offered me the job. I accepted the position.

I could see that God was opening doors for me. My schedule was from 6:00 a.m. until 2:00 p.m. I had to wear a white uniform and white shoes. Mother had some white uniforms, and her white shoes were too large, but I wore them anyway.

One month later, the school board called me to offer me the teacher assistant job. After careful thought, I turned it down because the hospital job was full-time, and the school job did not work during the summer months.

After seven years working in this position, I was offered a promotion as a coordinator. I worked in this position at the same hospital until retirement after twenty-eight years of service.

Throughout the years of living in our new home, I watched my children grow up right before my eyes. Each one of my children, except

Angela, was talented at playing sports. I watched my children develop physically, academically, socially, and spiritually. Their development was not without challenges along the way. There were a few academic challenges, but God graced my children the ability to overcome each challenge.

As a proud mother, I watched and shared many special moments in each of my children's lives. I saw each one of my children evolve from their childhood years to their teenage years and into adulthood. Throughout these developing years, I enjoyed celebrating their successes and how each obstacle pushed them into their preordained destiny. I was deeply proud to witness or hear of their acceptance of Jesus Christ into their lives and to see His power on display in them.

I took great enjoyment in watching my children excel in the different sports of their choosing. Each of my sons played Little League sports including baseball, football, and basketball. This experience encouraged them to venture into high school athletics. Kevin's love for baseball and his contribution as a pitcher was celebrated as his team won a state championship. Both twins played basketball for one year together. Kenneth ran cross country and played one year of football as a freshman in high school.

James Jr. was a very talented wrestler, baseball player, and cross-country runner in high school. James Jr.'s incredible talent in wrestling earned him the right to compete at the State Wrestling Tournament in his weight class. In high school baseball, James Jr. set a high school record. As a pitcher, he threw nineteen strikeouts in six innings with four strikeouts in one inning alone. James Jr. was very popular during his high school years and beyond. He was named Most Likely to Succeed, Outstanding Senior, Who's Who in America, and awarded the American Legion Award.

After high school, James Jr. was awarded a scholarship for college. Over a three-year period, he attended Christ for the Nations in pursuit of a Theology degree and Amarillo College in pursuit of a business management degree.

Juliet ran cross country and excelled in track and field. She earned numerous victories that earned her the right to compete in state level track and field competitions. Even though she did not win any state titles, she earned most valuable runner during her high school years of track and field. Juliet also played tennis for many years and continues to play today.

Jennifer was also a very good athlete also. She was named Most Valuable Player for softball during her senior year of high school. For her outstanding athleticism in softball, she was awarded a softball scholarship for college.

Milton was multitalented in almost everything that he set his heart to do. In high school, Milton exhibited leadership skills by serving as student council president and a member of Student Teacher Advisory Committee. He had a multitude of accomplishments in sports, beginning with state runner-up in weightlifting. In high school football, Milton led the team as captain of the football team, and he earned the title of All Conference four years in a row, All District four years in a row, and All State three years in a row. Milton was also highly gifted in the art of dance. He won numerous talent competitions and choreographed routines for the high school band's Pops Ensemble. Milton transitioned from high school to attending Florida State University in pursuit of a business major while playing football for the university for a couple of years.

Between the years 1975 through 1986, I was blessed to see each one of my children graduate from high school. Each one of them left high school and attended college. I know that if God had not devised a plan of escape from bondage, none of us may have lived long enough for me to write about.

Oral Roberts University

The twins were the first of my children to graduate from high school and go to college. Kevin and Kenneth spent the first two years at St. Johns River Community College working on their associate's degree. As the twins came close to the end of their two-year program, they looked for another college to further their education. One day, Kenneth saw an advertisement in the newspaper that Oral

Roberts University was having a seminar one weekend. The ad stated that room and board and food was included.

Kenneth took a bus to Oral Roberts University. When he arrived, Kenneth was so impressed that Kenneth wanted to study at ORU. He in turn convinced Kevin. ORU sent an application in the mail. We filled out the application in the mail and sent it back. The next news we received was they were both accepted. This was a miracle because we were very poor, and I did not have any money to send them to school.

The twins were awarded a grant to pay for their tuition, but they still needed transportation to get there. Kenneth and Kevin had to report to school on a certain date for orientation. I did not have any money and did not know how I was going to provide them with transportation. I asked Papa Albert to cosign with me to take out a loan to borrow the money. I explained to the company that I needed money for airfare and money for the twins to put in their pocket.

Next, I needed transportation to get the twins from Palatka to the airport in Jacksonville.

Betty, a lady who worked with me at the hospital, overheard me talking. She came to me and said that she would take us to the airport if I just give her some money for gas. That was all that she asked for. I asked her if she was sure, and she said yes. I had enough money left over from the loan to give her gas money. I gave Betty forty dollars, and she gave me twenty dollars back. Betty told me that she never knew when she may need help. I really appreciated her kindness.

We arrived in Jacksonville airport, and the twins made it in time to catch their plane. As the twins walked down the corridor to board their plane, tears started to flow down my face. I realized that this was the first time that I would be separated from them. I was happy for both, but at the same time, I felt a great sense of loss deep inside.

Both Kevin and Kenneth earned their bachelor's degrees from Oral Roberts University. Kenneth earned a Bachelor of Arts in biblical literature at Oral Roberts University, and as a graduate student at ORU School of Theology and Missions, he earned his Masters of Divinity degree. In January 1988, Kenneth entered the United States Army as an army chaplain. Kevin earned his Bachelor of Science in elementary education from Oral Roberts University and earned his Masters of School Administration Degree from Baruch College of the City University of New York. Kevin began his teaching career in 1982.

My New House

A few years later, I saw a Jim Walter Homes ad in the newspaper. The ad stated that Jim Walter Homes builds 80 percent of houses at no down payment. The land would serve as the collateral. I felt this was an opportunity to buy me a new home. I talked to Mother about this, and she did not think it was a good idea. She thought that I could not afford this. I told Mother that God will make a way. I also talked it over with my dad, who said, "Go for it. If you get slack with the payments, I will be your backup."

Daddy's encouragement was all that I needed to hear. I called the phone number from the ad, and a lady from Jim Walter Homes introduced herself and told me that she would come out to talk to me. She explained everything that they do. She explained that Jim Walters Homes will do 80 percent of the work building a new house. The lady explained to me that if I can get someone to complete the plumbing or electrical work, I would keep my overall costs to a minimum. I thought about my Uncle Roosevelt, so I called him and asked him if he would do the plumbing. I thought about letting Jim Walters complete the electrical work because I wanted to make sure that the electrical work was completed properly.

Uncle Roosevelt did the plumbing, and Jim Walters Homes completed the electrical work for me.

Uncle Roosevelt told me that it would cost about three hundred dollars for the plumbing work, and he would not charge me for his labor. However, Uncle Roosevelt said he needed me to pay for the parts. My dad spoke with his brother, Uncle Robert. Daddy told Uncle Robert to give Uncle Roosevelt the money for the parts. Daddy and

Uncle Robert paid Uncle Roosevelt for parts and also paid him for his labor.

After this, I found out that Jim Walters Homes had to complete 90 percent of the work rather than 80 percent that I was quoted because we lived within the city limits. Jim Walter Homes completed almost all the work with the exception of some small things. For example, Jim Walter Homes would not hang up the cabinets in the kitchen. Instead, my son James Jr. and a friend, Bill, hung up the cabinets. Bill did not charge me anything for his labor. I also needed racks to hang in the closets. A minister friend hung the racks for me, and he did not charge me anything. Not one person who performed labor in my house charged me for their labor. In the bathroom, I needed someone to install the shower and a special type of wall that I had to put up in the bathroom. One of my cousins, Claude, took care of this for me. He did not charge for his labor either.

God worked it out so that everything that I was required to complete was taken care of, and Jim Walter Homes took care of everything else. Another project that I needed was for my old house to be torn down. One day, a lady that I knew suggested for me to ask this man who worked in the neighborhood to tear down my house and let him keep the wood. She said if I let him keep the wood, he would not charge me.

I was happy to see my dream of owning a new house turn into reality. As the years passed by, I witnessed my children's transition into their adult lives. My heart was full of joy as my children finished college, got married, and started their own families. My household size continued to dwindle until there was no one left home but me. After seventeen years, I contacted an attorney and filed for divorce from James.

I met a man name Ernest that I dated for a couple of years until he asked me to marry him. In 1988, we were married at his house. I moved into his house, and I eventually sold my house. Through marriage, I was blessed with the addition of four wonderful stepchildren—Loretha, Nancy, Ernest Jr., and Wallace—whom I love as my very own children and who love me the same.

After my retirement, I enjoyed the opportunity to travel to various places. My children have blessed me by paying for all my travel expenses and more. I have traveled back to New York, Hawaii, Washington, Arizona, Texas, North Carolina, and Delaware. Some of these places I have traveled to more than once since retirement. I am very grateful to God for the blessing of children and family. I am extremely grateful to God for reuniting me with Thelma and Dot. They have helped me through the difficult times and have shared my good times. Their love for me and my children has never wavered once in my lifetime.

Daddy's Illness

In 1999, I retired from my job at the hospital after twenty-eight years. It was during the same year that my dad started getting sick. Mom had already passed away in 1991, and I became concerned about his well-being. Since Kevin had moved back to New York, we agreed that it would be better for Kevin to move into Daddy's house so that he would not be alone. I felt better knowing that someone was there for him. After several months had passed, I made a trip to New York to take care of Daddy so that Kevin and his wife Edith could have a break. I took care of Daddy in New York for about three months before returning to Florida.

As Daddy got older, his health and mental status became an issue. In 2000, Daddy came to visit me in Florida, and I noticed that his memory was deteriorating. There were times that he would walk away from the house and get lost. My children and I decided that it would be best for him to remain in Florida so that I could care for him better. I was happy to care for my dad because he was always taking care of me. He was the best dad in the world to me. I cared for my dad for nearly five years until his Alzheimer's worsened to a point where I needed extra help. It was in 2005 when I heard Dad from bedroom saying,

"Help me." I ran into the room and saw that he was stuck, trying to climb out of the window. At this point I knew that he needed care around the clock. I did not enjoy the thought of placing my dad in a nursing home, but he needed around-the-clock care. My children and I searched for a nursing home that would provide him with quality care that feels like home and allows him to retain his dignity. In 2005, we placed Daddy in a nursing home close to my home. My children and I and other family members were able to visit him often so that he would never feel neglected. We were very pleased with the excellent care that the nursing home provided him up to his death in 2007.

When Daddy's condition became worse, I did not want to leave his side. With the support of my daughters, Angela and Jennifer, we sat by his side up until he took his last breath. My dad was a mighty man of God. He not only loved the Lord with all his heart, but he also modeled Christ as a father, a husband, a grandfather, a wonderful brother, and a friend. His life passage from the Bible was Psalms 8, which exemplifies God's excellence. Daddy strongly believed in the supremacy of God. He was loved by everyone who knew him. I will never forget my daddy because he taught me how to love through his demonstration.

This was a sad and difficult time for me. The man who I call Daddy was an amazing father and a true man of God. He was there when I came into the world, and he left his mark on my life and on my children's lives forever. I thank God for allowing me to sit by his side as he transitioned to heaven, where I know that I will run to him when I see him again.

Mother's Illness

In 2006, Mother started getting sick. There were times when both Mother and Daddy were sick and at the hospital at the same time. Daddy was in the hospital here in Palatka with congested heart failure, and Mother was in the hospital in St. Augustine with a heart condition. For the next three years following Daddy's death, taking care of Mother's health became a full-time job at times, I spent weeks at her small apartment, and other times I had her brought to our house. I cooked her food and ran errands to pick up personal items and medication for her. We celebrated her ninetieth birthday by giving her a party at our church with all her family and friends. This a special day because God promised her ninety years and this birthday marked the fulfillment of His promise.

After her birthday, I continued to care for Mother as she fought aging and declining health. She was rushed to the emergency room numerous times. There were several times that we thought we lost her, but the doctors were able to revive her. Each one of these times, I had to face the hard reality that I would not have Mother forever. I became more concerned about Mother's health. At times, Mother insisted on going back to her apartment, so I decided to sleep over with her. Sometimes I kept her at our home, and other times I remained with her at her apartment.

On one occasion while I was at her apartment, I noticed Mother was in the bathroom for a long time. I kept asking her if she was okay. I heard her in a very faint voice say, "Help me." I ran into the bathroom and noticed that her speech was slurred. My first thought was that she had suffered a stroke. I called 911, and the paramedics came quickly. She was taken to the hospital immediately. Thelma came to help me clean up Mother's accident in the bathroom, and I told her, "Let's take care of her first, and I will come back later to clean the apartment."

The doctors confirmed that Mother had a light stroke. She was kept in the hospital for three weeks. The doctor told me that Mother had too many problems for me to be able to care for her by myself. The doctor ordered rehabilitation for Mother at the rehab wing of the nursing home. Mother remained in the rehab wing for two months, and then she told me that she felt it was better for her to remain at the nursing home rather than go back to her apartment. She was concerned that she would be too much of a burden on me. The staff moved her out of the rehab wing to another wing of the nursing home.

At this point, Mother told me to give away all her possessions. She insisted that I did not sell anything. My children and I followed her instructions and moved her belongings out of her apartment. Mother remained at the nursing home until her health turned for the worse. At this point, she was rushed to the hospital.

With rapidly declining health, Mother inspired all of us to love God and love each other.

Over the next twenty-five days, I did not know if Mother would make it to the next day. Thelma, Dot, and I spent all day and some nights by her side. We were blessed by the support of many family members and friends who spent quality time with Mother and made sure our daily needs were met.

This was a very difficult time for the three of us, but she was my mother, and she was their sister. This woman of God was so full of love. I cannot forget her favorite scripture. Her life verse comes from 2 Chronicles 7:14 KJV, which states,

"If my people which are called by my name, shall humble themselves and pray, and seek my face, and turn from their wicked ways; then will I hear from heaven and will heal their land."

In Mother's final days, Thelma, Dot, and I remained by her side up to her last breath. Before she departed into eternity, this mighty woman of God passed the baton to us to continue running the race in spreading the gospel of Christ.

As I reflect over the life of my mother and father, I can only give glory to God for blessing me with such wonderful loving parents. My parents loved me and my children in such an amazing way. My children and I continue to reminisce over the wonderful times that we shared with Daddy, Mother, and Mom. My parents laid a solid foundation for me and my children, and we are better because of them. I truly admired the relationship between the three of them. There was never a time for bitterness or strife between them.

As I continue to walk in the path that God had placed in front of me, I am amazed by His faithfulness, His love, and His compassion. I can honestly say that I have experienced many storms and many good times in my life. Through each storm, God has brought me through as precious gold.

He continues to refine the impurities out of my life so that I can shine the light of Christ in such a dark world.

I would like to take a moment to describe some of the many good times. To list all of the good times would be quite lengthy. Nevertheless,

I can clearly say that some of the most wonderful times in my life have been with my children and family. We are a very close-knit family, and we draw our strength from each other and our Heavenly Father. The strength of my family becomes very evident during our family gatherings, our celebrations, and during times of sorrow or hardship. It is during these times of laughter, crying, and thanking God that I consider some of our best of times.

From the time we were in New York, we came together as a family around the dining room and kitchen table. It is here that we grew closer. James had a way of interrupting these great times, but he was unable to destroy the glue that God used to bind our hearts together. My children and I continue to gather around my dining table to talk and catch up on the affairs of our lives. On holidays and special events, we come together to celebrate and enjoy a good meal. So often laughter becomes the call of the day. Our conversations sometimes last for hours with little regard for time. Everyone feels at home and free to share their heart on a matter without the pain of judgment.

Over the years, my children and close family members have blessed me in tremendous ways. From monetary gifts to my heart's desire, I'm always overwhelmed with the expression of their love toward me. Over the past forty-four years, my children have afforded me the opportunity to travel to numerous places throughout the country. All my travels have been shared with my children or very close family members and friends.

One of my fondest memories was my two-week vacation trip to Hawaii. My son Kenneth and his former wife Anna invited me to spend my vacation with them. This trip was so amazing that I could have easily been mistaken for a celebrity. My plane ride and my entire stay on the island had the makings of a red-carpet event. On the airplane, the stewardess collected money from the passengers for a raffle. Because I didn't have proper change, a passenger sitting next to me gave me money to put into the raffle. To my surprise, I was one of two people who won the money raffle.

When I arrived on the island, Anna and one of her friends took me shopping to one of the largest flea markets that I had ever seen.

The flea market was located in a stadium. Anna and her friend vowed that we should shop until we drop. I could not keep up with them, so I found a chair and sat down until they were finished.

After the shopping was over, Kenneth and Anna took me to a Hawaiian luau. This was the first time that I had experienced such a welcoming event. During the luau, the Hawaiians placed a beautiful flowery garland around my neck, a long-standing tradition in Hawaii. A pig was roasted underground, and the dancers performed the hula dance for the newcomers. All the grandmothers were asked to come to the stage to honor us. I didn't want to go, but Kenneth and Anna persuaded me to go forward. While on stage, I was told that I would have to kiss a hundred men. This was interesting. So many men in line, and I don't see my way out of this. I had to kiss all those men. I also tried to do the hula dance. I had a lot of fun, even though I never mastered the hula dance and grew tired from kissing so many men.

After the luau, Kenneth and Anna took me to some of the different islands in Hawaii.

Afterward, we went to see Pearl Harbor. As part of a tour, we were taken inside a building and shown a movie of how Pearl Harbor was attacked. Next, we were taken by boat to visit the *Arizona* Memorial. The names of all the soldiers who died in the attack on Pearl Harbor were etched into the walls. In the middle of the floor there was a see-through glass pane.

When we looked through the glass, we saw bits and pieces of the destroyed ship. Oil was still leaking from the boat, and no one was able to figure out why. Kenneth then took me to a very small submarine that survived the attack. I tried to figure out how men were able to survive in such a small submarine. I learned so much on this trip. Kenneth and Anna and I also went to see a couple of movies, and we also spent Mother's Day in church together.

My vacation isn't over yet. A few days later, Kenneth and Anna rented a cottage at the beach for three days. We spent some of the most relaxing days at the beach. Everything was so beautiful. The weather was just right. The atmosphere was filled with peace and solitude. I used the time to read and enjoy God's beautiful creation. I could not stop talking about this trip when I returned home.

Another trip that I really enjoyed was when my son Kevin gave me a trip to New York for the weekend. Kevin and I toured the city. We took in a Broadway show, a Yankees baseball game, and we went to a church banquet. I will never forget this trip because I had so much fun. This was one of the best weekends that I can remember.

I could easily talk all day about all the wonderful times that I had with all my children on my trips. I have been so blessed to fly to Dallas a couple of times and West Virginia to spend time with James and his wife Gwenneth. Juliet and I traveled together to meet James in Arizona to attend Kenneth's army promotional award ceremony for Army Colonel. I traveled with Angela, James Jr, Juliet, Jennifer, and Milton to Columbus Georgia, North Carolina, New York, Wilmington, Delaware, and more.

All these trips were wonderful and entertaining. As a family, we have always found a way to turn a long trip into an exciting adventure. I have also traveled on several trips with my husband Ernest. We spent time together with his family in Seattle, Washington, and Key West, Florida. His family treated us as royalty. My travels continue to provide me with quality time with my family.

Our good times also included weddings, graduations, birthdays, and church events. Nothing can describe the joy in my heart than that of knowing that all of my children have accepted Christ as their personal Savior.

I cannot leave out the most important and joyous moments in my life, which are times spent in the presence of the Lord. I am so grateful to God for allowing me to see his glory magnified in the lives of my sons and daughters. I never would have imagined that I would become the mother of preachers, teachers, singers, and servants who are committed to following the command given by Jesus in Mark 16:15, KJV which states, "Go ye into all the world, and preach the gospel to every creature."

Nothing can compare to the times that I have spent sitting at the feet of my children preaching, teaching, and sharing the gospel of Christ. As a mother, wife, grandmother, and Sunday school teacher, my focus is clear. I was made in the image of our Heavenly Father to praise and give him glory. My life has taken many unexpected turns, but I can truly say that each turn was ordained by God to point me to my next duty station. I have not always understood the reason for the pain and suffering. There were times in which I questioned God and wondered how long before He would rescue me. However, I can say that God has never been late or absent in my life.

I am so grateful that God has blessed me with wonderful children, stepchildren, grandchildren, and greatgrandchildren. Over the years, my family has blossomed into a beautiful tree planted by the river of life.

CHAPTER 10

New Revelations

There were a few things that were brought to my attention after we left New York and were living in Florida. None of the information was good. Our landlady in South Ozone Park Mrs. Terry told me that James left the house in a very bad condition. She said that James punched holes in the walls and painted all the rooms black. The Terrys were very good people, and they did not deserve this type of treatment in their house. They had an enormous amount of repair work that had to be done to bring the house back to livable condition. I felt so bad because there was nothing that I could do to help.

James Moves to Detroit

One of James's sisters, Laura Ann, wrote a letter to me, informing me of some events that happened after we left. In her letter, Laura Ann told me approximately six to seven months after we left New York that James asked me to come to Detroit to live with her. James's perception of reality was distorted. She went on to say that James had started beating her children and calling her children by our children's names. She had to stop him from beating her children a few times. Laura Ann began to realize that there was something wrong with this picture. After Laura Ann saw her brother talking to himself and no one else was in the room, she realized something was wrong with James.

Because of James's bizarre behavior, Laura Ann made an appointment with a doctor to have him examined. At the appointment, the psychiatrist diagnosed James with a mental disorder and admitted him to an assisted living home. Laura Ann could not remember the exact diagnosis, but I found out later that he suffered from paranoia and schizophrenia.

Assisted living homes were sometimes used in lieu of large hospitals to care for the mentally ill patients. Assisted living facilities for mental health offer a more structured environment that focuses on promoting sustained healing.

For James, the assisted living home would allow him the opportunity to contribute to his treatment and progress with the supportive help of the medical staff and other residents.

Laura Ann signed the papers for James to live in one of the assisted living homes, and the doctor monitored his progress.

James was not kept in the home for a long period.

However, during his stay in the assisted home, James met a woman who also suffered from a mental illness, and the two of them developed a relationship. I do not know the exact length of time that James spent in the assisted living home. At some point, James and the woman rented a place together. According to Laura Ann, both James and the woman received social security income because of their mental illness.

Out of this relationship, two children were born. One was born in October, and the younger was born nine months later the following year. Laura Ann cared for both baby girls until the youngest started walking. According to Laura Ann, she had three children of her own and was also caring for James's two young children. James and the woman had asked Laura Ann to care for the children because they were unable to fully care for their two children.

Caring for five children had become very challenging, especially since Laura had a heart condition. When the woman asked Laura Ann to care for the two baby girls on a full-time basis, Laura Ann told her if she would give her about a month to rest her heart, she would take care of them on a more permanent basis. The woman and James came and picked up both children and took them to their home. Without notice, Laura Ann said the woman left with the children and went to Louisiana. Laura Ann was upset and confronted James by saying,

"I told you to give me about a month and I would take the children permanently for you."

Shortly after the woman left, James followed suit by going to Louisiana to be with the woman and his two youngest children. I never truly understood the entire story of what happened between James and this woman in Louisiana. My son James Jr. shared some information with me that he found out years later. He claimed that the woman had some serious health conditions and passed away while living in Louisiana. I do not know who the person was, but someone took care of the two girls. My children are communicating with their half-sisters.

James's Death

My children told me that James spoke with Angela, Milton, James, and Juliet before his death. Angela said that she spoke with her dad three times, Juliet once, James Jr. once, and Milton visited him and spoke with him a few times. Milton, my youngest child, went to see his father after he received information of his whereabouts. Since Milton's visit, James called Milton regularly, asking for money to buy food. Milton sent money to his dad almost every other week to help him out.

Afterward, Angela asked for James's phone number from Milton. James asked Angela, "Will you forgive me."

"I forgive you."

"I'm sorry for what I did. I was not in my right mind."

Next, Angela proceeded to walk her dad through the sinner's prayer. Immediately, he told her that he already knew the Lord. During one of the conversations, James started asking her questions about me. Angela assured her father that I had already forgiven him a long time ago.

About one year before James died, my husband Ernest told me that a man with a deep voice called our house, wanting to speak to me. After Ernest described his voice, I confirmed that it was my ex-husband, James, who had called. Juliet also told me that she was shocked when James called her house to speak to her. She said he spoke with her husband at that time, and she only spoke briefly with him.

It was about two months prior to his death when James's brother Robert called James Jr. and told him that he needs to call his dad. James Jr. called his dad and spoke to him.

According to James Jr., his dad said that he was the last one to talk to him. James was so glad to hear his son's voice and was very remorseful for his actions in the past.

James then said, "I am no longer on that side of the track. I gave my life to the Lord." This was good news to James Jr. "I have already forgiven you."

Kevin, Kenneth and Jennifer did not have any contact with their father before he passed.

It was 1994, approximately one week after Milton's last contact with James, when a neighbor stopped by to check on James. The neighbor found James unresponsive. The neighbor saw Milton's work phone number on James's nightstand and called Milton's job to notify him of James's condition. Milton immediately called me to tell me that James was dying and gave me the phone number of the intensive care unit at the hospital. I was a bit hesitant, but I picked up the phone and started to dial the phone number to the hospital, but I did not go through with it. Shortly after, Milton called me again and told me that he had passed.

After James passed, Robert called James Jr. to notify him of his death. The cause of death was pancreatic cancer. Next, all the children were notified. Prior to the funeral, Kevin and James Jr. went to their father's apartment to pick up a suit to bury him in. Because they did not have a key, James Jr. thought that it would be easy to break in through the window. This turned out to be a bad idea because James had bolted the windows securely with screws.

There was no way that someone could have broken into his apartment. Kevin and James Jr. could clearly see the severity of his paranoia. They had to get a key from someone to let them in. They found a bunch of medicine and tissue and blood throughout his apartment.

All our children except Kenneth were able to go to the funeral. According to our children, the funeral was very sad. There was only one other person outside of the Revell family who came to the funeral. It was at the funeral that our children met Suzanne and Tonya, James other two daughters, for the first time. I did not go to the funeral.

The Banquet Retold

I have mentioned the incident that happened in Brooklyn the night of my church banquet. Immediately after I walked through the front door, James accused me of spending time with another man. I was picked up and dropped off by Mr. and Mrs. Hacker. When I returned home, James ripped my beautiful red dress off of me right in front of my children.

He then told the children, "Look at your mother!"

I was in a state of shock and totally humiliated to the point that I blocked this out of my mind for years. As I mentioned in an earlier chapter, this memory came flooding back while I was watching a movie. In this movie, the abuse inflicted on a woman by her fiancé brought back the painful night of the banquet.

It was only a few weeks after this that my oldest daughter Angela told me what happened on the night of my church banquet. I am not going to go into specific details, but I will say that James not only violated our wedding vows, but he also violated his own daughter too. Something inside of me shattered into pieces. It felt like my heart stopped beating from the shocking blow of what happened that night. I was stunned, gasping for the right response. I started to think about the pain that Angela had suffered for all these years. She was a little girl, and I felt like I failed to protect her. I never could have imagined this happening because I never imagined James ever crossing this line.

As Angela provided details of this night, my memory started to return, and I realized that I must have walked in on something catching James off guard. His immediate reaction was to humiliate me and accuse me of destroying any possibility of me finding out or questioning what really was going on. I was so shaken up by what was brought to light that my emotions were torn apart. I was both deeply heartbroken for Angela and fiercely angry with James.

One day after we arrived in Florida, Angela told me that her dad had done something to her, but she never gave me a clue that it was of this nature. I found out later that she was angry with me for not protecting her, but I never knew any of this. Angela did not reveal to me what happened until about a month ago while writing this book. She kept this from me because she did not want to hurt me. My response to her was, "Don't worry about me. I am already hurt. I am more concerned about you. You need to be free from this pain that you have carried all these years."

I will be honest in saying that this news shook me up so much that it was hard not to feel both betrayed by James and angry for my daughter's sake. This is something that only the blood of Jesus can heal. I had to reach deep inside and allow the Holy Spirit to touch my most sensitive places and bring healing. I am confident that Jesus died for this too. I strongly believe that as He bore our sins on the cross, He also felt our pain. I believe that each stripe that He took on our behalf holds our healing. I continue to encourage Angela to trust God, and He will heal her. I believe that she and I will one day be able to help someone else in the same situation.

Life in the Revell Household

The thought came across my mind a few times about what life was like for James growing up in the Revell household. I wondered if there was a connection between James's anger issues, his alcoholic abuse and his physically abusive nature to me and to our children. I thought about some of the things that he shared with me about his life before we met.

To make the connection between James's childhood and his life as an adult I had to ask his family members for information about James earlier years and the household environment of the Revell home. In response to the information that I received from his siblings Robert and Laura Ann let's take a trip back in time to the Revell home. First, we will look at James as a boy growing up in North Carolina, and second, we will look at the home environment including his parents and siblings. James's parents, Hugh Sr. and Carrie, gave birth to sixteen children but only nine lived beyond a couple of years of age.

There was more than one set of twins in which James was the third oldest child that was born and lived. Not all the twins lived beyond a couple of years of age. As a teen, James was described as quiet, friendly, well-mannered but not a very talkative person. James was an introvert. Sometimes James was found mumbling to himself and smiling. James was not a leader but a follower, often standing off by himself.

Realizing his physical strength, quite often he would hurt someone playing or kidding around. He had friends and wasn't a total loner as some introverts were. He often saw himself as the black sheep and not receiving as much care as the rest of the siblings. He could be very forceful if someone crossed him.

James graduated from Calvin Scott Brown High School in Winston, North Carolina.

Some of his hobbies included baseball, going to the movies, fishing, and hanging out with friends. One of his main strengths was his incredible physical strength. He was as strong as an ox. He would show off his strength by lifting tractors, cars, arm wrestling, and so on. It is sad that no one recognized his weightlifting and wrestling abilities.

His weakness was drinking and low self-esteem. Sometimes anger was detected, and it spewed out from James. His brother Robert said that he remembers arguments about work responsibilities not being equally assigned, and James felt that Robert knew that he was being treated unfairly. James had some very close friends. One friend was his cousins Agnes Wood, Shirley Moore, Alvania Myrick, and Bernard Freeman. These five cousins were very close and went to school together.

The Revell home environment was family oriented. The family lived on a farm on which all the children shared the responsibilities of working in the fields together. Weekends normally consist of a lot of drinking and, at some point, card playing and bootlegging.

That's when the arguing and fighting usually started, more so during the months after the harvest was in, until the annual profits were depleted. This was typical, from Friday to Sunday James's father, Hugh Sr., was also more of an introvert. He did not talk much. He kept his feelings inside and did not play until he was pushed to a breaking point; then he was very dangerous. Though he kept quiet, when he talked, he meant what he said and said what he meant.

He was a good-looking man who drunk a lot at times and rarely went to church. The ladies admired his complexion and his hair. He seemed to have cared more for the girls than the boys, which was exemplified with his grandchildren. The exception to that was that he appeared to have shown favoritism to the boys and girls with lighter complexion.

James's mother, Carrie, was more of an extrovert. She talked more than James's dad and made friends easily. She didn't mind letting you know in a nice way that you hurt her. She was the one who kept the family together in the pathway of righteousness. Although when she was on her drinking spree, she didn't go to church often, but she made sure that we still went to church. Carrie was very warm, loving, and attractive. When she was on a drinking spree, she and her cousin would sneak off at nights on weekends to go to the club and the bootleg joint through the woods. She enjoyed singing, especially the Hymns of Zion, cooking, and traveling. She would sing hymns as she cooked and worked. She loved the Lord, and many times at night, the children could hear her praying to the Lord and singing those hymns.

When all the crops were in and there was no money, she would find jobs working in the houses of the local whites to earn money to feed the family, buy clothes and shoes for the children, in addition to supplementing the family needs during the times of working the crops. She had the gift of bringing the family together. She regularly displayed her skills of gathering, planning, and organizing, and she was extremely talented in food preparation.

On the other hand, James's father Hugh Sr. was industrious and skillful with his hands, and he possessed enormous physical strength. After receiving this information from Robert I can see where much of the behavior exhibited from James stemmed from.

In terms of their parents' treatment of the children, they loved each and every one of them equally, as per Robert's point of view. However, there were feelings that the lighter complexion siblings were treated better by both parents than the darker complexion ones. Robert said that he never noticed that, except when it came to his oldest brother and middle sister. For whatever reason, they seemed to have their way. Nevertheless, Robert felt that he was included in having favor, not because of complexion, but because they saw him as being smart and intelligent. James always complained about being treated unequally by the older ones. In all honesty, Robert said he doesn't know if that was because of his complexion or his temperament and personality.

Both of James's parents engaged in destructive behavior that was demonstrated in front of their children and reaped very harmful consequences in the lives of their children. The mere notion of favoring one child over another child can initiate devastating long-term effects on a child. The negative effects can bring about an ongoing sense of worthlessness, bouts of depression, and can hamper family relationships and intimate relationships with other people.

I remember the look in James's face when he would talk about how his parents favored some of the other siblings over him. This apparently had a lasting effect on him. I can also see how easy it was for James to get hooked on alcohol. He grew up in a dysfunctional environment with alcohol abuse and physical abuse centered at the core.

When James and I were dating, he mentioned that his father would carelessly throw his very young children up in the air in front of his mother. His mother's maternal instincts would cause her to reach out to catch the child before he or she is dropped. His father could not see the danger or seriousness of the situation. It was obvious that he did not value the sanctity of life and often ignored his wife's cry to save her babies. My heart would tremble when James described these frightening incidents, but he too repeated the same behavior.

The behavior demonstrated in front of the Revell children, the preferential treatment based on skin color and hair texture along with James's mental illness all contributed to the James that I married and came to know. I can now link the relationship between James's early years in the Revell household and how this type of behavior and depraved attitudes transferred into his adult life. James repeated many of the same behavior that he saw portrayed by his parents. The only exception was that James was also schizophrenic, which added another frightening element to the equation.

However, I do believe that James's resentment for his parents' preference of one child over another and the alcohol abuse affected James more than some of his other siblings. I can clearly say that God has broken the generational curse of alcoholism and physical violence from being passed down to our children. Over the years, I have been asked which one of my children is my favorite. I gladly respond, "No one." I love all my children equally. I have always valued each one of my children as a wonderful blessing to my life. We should all see our children the way that God sees them as precious in His sight.

CHAPTER 11

To God Be the Glory!

The Devil Failed to Take Us Out!

There have been numerous times that I have asked the Lord, "Why me?" I tried to figure out what was really taking place in our lives. I was sometimes confused because of James's alcohol abuse and his erratic and very violent behavior. I did not know when he started drinking and what caused him to turn to alcohol. I didn't understand how he could turn so violent when he was drinking like a person completely out of control, but when someone threatened to call the police, he had enough sense to stop.

At times, James's behavior seemed like that of a mental disorder. Many times, he could not distinguish between reality and fantasy. Often, James acted paranoid; he would close the blinds and make the house extremely dark because he believed that someone was watching him. I never understood how he claimed that he saw footprints on the sidewalk or was able to know that strangers across the street were talking about him.

When James was not drinking, such as during the nine-month period that he stopped drinking, we all noticed his behavior appeared calmer and more rational. He made more sense when he spoke. When he was drinking heavily, he struggled to complete a thought, and his behavior was erratic and very destructive. Looking at James's patterns of irrational behavior, I was led to believe that his behavior was primarily tied to alcohol. I was still confused by his ability to turn off the abuse at will and his paranoia tendencies.

I did not find out that James was diagnosed with paranoid schizophrenia until years later while in Florida. This explains his paranoia, delusions, and hallucinations, but I'm left with the question of why he had not shown any signs of this disorder while we were dating. Was he hiding his mental illness from me? If so, was he taking medication, and did he at some point stop taking it? I still did not understand how he could turn his violent behavior off the way that you turn off a light switch. This caused me to ask more questions, research domestic abusers, and alcohol addictions from a spiritual point of view.

What God has revealed to me was that James suffered from severe paranoid schizophrenia and alcoholism and that he was an abusive husband. What I had failed to see was that demons and evil spirits pounce on people with mental illness and addictions such as alcohol addictions and schizophrenia. This is more pronounced in extreme cases such as with James.

Demonic influence is a powerful force that exists in the spirit world. There is constant spiritual warfare in the spirit world, which is the cause of nearly all calamities seen in our world today. The battle of good versus evil is real and should not be ignored. The demonic influence is so powerful that it dominates a person so strongly that the demon or evil spirit can take complete control (possession) or strongly influence behavior. Demonic influence is the unseen force causing the behavior while the person's mind is too weak to fight.

Without Christ residing inside of us, we lack the protection against such evil forces, and we do not have the power in our own strength to defeat it.

In James's case, he was not saved, and his paranoid schizophrenic condition combined with alcohol addiction served as a catalyst for the enemy to create a foothold into his life. After speaking with some of James's siblings, I gathered that James had some resentment and anger issues from earlier years. Before we got married, James complained about always getting hand-me-downs from his older siblings. He also complained that some of his siblings were given preferential treatment over him. These feelings of resentment, jealousy, and anger lay dormant, creating a foothold for the enemy to pounce on.

Ephesians 4:25–27 (KJV) states, "Wherefore putting away lying, speak every man truth with his neighbour: for we are members one of another. Be ye angry, and sin not: let not the sun go down upon your wrath: Neither give place to the devil. Let him that stole steal no more: but rather let him labour, working with his hands the thing, which is good, that he may have to give to him that needeth."

This passage of scripture clearly instructs us how to behave when we are confronted with something that goes against God's word or something that we disagree with. It goes a little further instructing us not to give place to the devil. In other words, do not allow the devil any opportunity to tempt us, to succumb to temptations that will cause us to take pleasure in ill thoughts toward someone. In other words, do not think about or consider retaliating or taking revenge in a matter. When we react in this manner, we open the floodgates for the enemy to rage war against us.

I do not know how much resentment, anger, and jealousy James carried inside him, but I do know that he spoke about this with deep feelings. However, God has shown me the importance of being filled with the Holy Spirit and staying close to him. We by ourselves do not have the power to overcome the devil. We need the spirit of Christ dwelling within us to resist sin or the temptation to engage in the suggestions offered by the devil may cause us to give into sin. In James's case, I believe that James not only gave in to the temptations of sin, but he made it easy for the devil to turn a foothold into a huge doorway. By the addition of alcohol abuse, mental illness, and the lack of the Holy Spirit, James became easy prey.

I believe that the devil knew or at least suspected that God had a special purpose for my life and for my children's lives. The devil used James to launch a full attack on us. He attacked our minds through physical beatings to keep us in place. He did this to establish fear so enormous that any thought of leaving would seem too dangerous to attempt.

He attacked me mentally by filling my ears with negative thoughts such as "God doesn't hear you" or "God will not help you. No one wants you with all those children."

With all the hell the devil launched against us, God remained in complete control. He allowed the devil to push me and my children to our knees so that we could cry out to Him. Out of desperation for our lives, I cried out, and God answered me. He was answering me all along, but I failed to discern His voice because the enemy was filling my ears with doom and gloom.

When I started to read His word and learn more about Him, I began to clearly discern the voice of the Lord. With the help of the Lord, I was able to hear God say, "This is not for you, and I will help you." God was faithful to His word and delivered us from bondage. I am here today in my right mind because of God's grace and mercy in our time of need. I am a living witness to say that the devil failed to take us out.

My Children Successes

I must say that I am very proud of all my children's successes throughout their lives. No one but God could have written and orchestrated such a storyline called our life. This nonfiction autobiographical story begins as a beautiful romance story that quickly turns violent and becomes a battle for survival.

With God's mighty hand of deliverance, freedom is granted, and a new life begins. God has so richly blessed my life and my children's lives. Because of Christ, Kevin has been teaching in New York City public schools for thirty-two years. He and his beautiful wife Edith, also a teacher, are the parents of a beautiful daughter, Kendra.

The other twin, Kenneth, served in the army for twenty-eight years. Kenneth currently holds the ranking of Colonel and US Army chaplain. He has earned numerous awards and decorations. Since his enlistment into the army, Kenneth has been stationed in several locations including Fort Bragg in North Carolina, Fort Benning in Georgia, Fort Huachuca in Arizona, and Iraq. He is currently command chaplain for the Ninety-Fourth Air Missile Defense Command in Honolulu, Hawaii. His accomplishments in the US Army are too many to put into print. Kenneth was married to the late Anna N. Hilliard for twenty-eight years until she went home to the Lord on August 2014. They adopted one son, Chris (nephew), and have two grandsons, Christian and Brandon.

As an ordained minister of the gospel, Kenneth possesses superb oratorical skills and continues to preach and spread the gospel of Christ to every place that the Lord sends him. No one would have known that he did not learn to read until the eighth grade. This would not be possible if Jesus did not intervene and deliver us from bondage. Kenneth developed a love of Christ at a very young age while we were still in New York. This relationship has emerged into a powerful union, leaving his mark every place he enters.

My oldest daughter, Angela, and her husband Ronnie reside in Palatka and are the parents of one son Alfred and the grandparents of Elyissia and Toriyanna Angela teaches at St. Johns River State College as a computer professor. Angela has earned several degrees and certifications including an associate degree and Bachelors in Accounting degree, a Bachelors in Information Systems degree, a masters in information science degree. Just recently, she received a doctorate in education degree. I was so proud of Angela for achieving such a high accomplishment. My eyes were filled with tears of joy as she was bestowed the title of doctor in her profession. James Jr. has earned a number of business accomplishments. Some of his business ventures include CEO of Thunder Rock, his own bottled water company, and he worked as a manager for Omnitrition. James Jr. was the first black manager hired by the company and later became a district manager. James Jr. was responsible for setting up warehouses throughout various regions.

Omnitrition presented James Jr. with the Most Helpful award for his outstanding work on behalf of the company. In West Virginia, the United Parcel Service (UPS) gave James Jr. an award for his hard work in servicing the largest account in the Kanawha Valley area.

Juliet has earned a Bachelor of Science in Business Management degree and a Master's in Business Administration degree and is also a teacher and a writer. She has taught high school business education for the past couple of years. Prior to teaching, Juliet worked in the business industry for more than twenty years. She is the mother of three children, Terry, Fylesha and Necolle, and resides in Jacksonville, Florida.

Jennifer resides in Palatka and has worked at Georgia Pacific for the past fourteen years and is the mother of two sons, Paris and Brandon. She also has one grandson, Paris Jr. I am so grateful to Jennifer for her willingness to go beyond the call of duty to assist me with my daily needs. She serves as a tremendous support to me.

Milton, my youngest child, has also accomplished much in the area of business. Milton has a long history of working in management in the automotive sales industry for more than twenty years. Milton currently works in insurance for Allstate. He and his wife, Sharon, both reside in Jacksonville, Florida, and they are the parents of one daughter, Britney, and two sons, Roy and Milton Jr.

I am not bragging about my children but rather on my Heavenly Father in the way He scripted our lives. When we were in New York under the horrendous abuse of James, I could not see beyond a day in front of me. In later years, my children have been very open in voicing how scared they were. Kevin describes our bondage as "sitting at death's door" each day. At times, my children felt that the only way that we would experience freedom was that someone would die. My children felt that James would kill all of us or we could have killed him. I was deeply saddened to hear how deep the wounds of abuse scarred their minds and their hearts.

I saw some of the effects left on my children and it scared me. For example, James Jr. went through a terrible period of anger and hostility toward his dad shortly after we arrived in Florida. James Jr. was so full of rage and anger toward his dad that I believe if he was in physical proximity of his dad, he would have killed him. James Jr. verbalized that he wanted to take a baseball bat and beat his dad across the head.

James Jr. had years of anger built up inside of him that began to spill over into almost everything that he did.

He started getting into fights at school. It's sad that my children experienced nothing but violence and fear from their dad. James taught his children not to bow down or back down to anyone. James could not see how his immoral teachings would endanger his children or cause his children to inflict harm on others. For some reason, James Sr. used James Jr. more often as a victim to impose his evil ideas. I am happy to say that James Jr.'s life changed drastically for the better. After he came to grips with reality, he began to see the built-up anger and hostility for his dad was similar to poison that is eating away at his total being. Poison eats away until the person or organism is fully destroyed. If James Jr. continued the same path, the outcome would have been deadly.

I thank God for delivering my son from the poison used by the enemy to destroy his life. James Jr.'s life has changed so much that he focuses his life on meeting the needs of the lost and disenfranchised and keeping his family connected. James Jr. has such a huge heart that he is often described as one who will give the shirt off his back to anyone in need. I have seen him display the love of Christ to many people. His heart is genuine, his actions are true, and his goals are to share the good news of Christ to those who crosses his path.

All my children have been physically and emotionally scarred by child abuse. Physical abuse usually heals sooner than emotional abuse. Emotional abuse cannot always be seen, but the scars often affect every part of the victim's life. I have seen the emotional scars left on Angela. The abuse inflicted on Angela left a very deep and painful scar that only Jesus can heal.

Throughout Angela's life, she has battled low self-esteem and bouts of depression. I have also seen how the pain of abuse has affected her personal relationships with men and her inability to say no to people. Angela is a very loving woman with a giving heart and desire to please the people around her. I strongly believe the pain from her father has impeded her ability to live a wholesome life.

As I write this book, I find that revisiting the painful tale of our past has brought answers to some questions and an awareness of some situations, which has opened the door for God to heal our wounds. My children and I had blocked out many of the painful events without realizing it. As we journey down memory lane, God has brought back some memories so that we can walk in the victory that Jesus has delivered us. I was crushed by the revelation of what happened to Angela. My heart was torn into pieces about events that were revealed to me years after arriving in Florida and several events revealed during the writing of this book. As a mother, I hurt when my children are hurt. I would give my life for my children.

Considering the recent revelation of events, I asked several questions, "Why did I not see these things? How could I have better protected my children?" As my anger started intensifying, I realized that God kept me from seeing this because He knew that I would have literally killed him for committing such acts on our children. If I had killed James, I would have blood on my hands, and my children would have had to live without their mother and father. Just the mere thought of my children being left without both parents would have devastated me.

There were numerous emotional battles that my children had to overcome. Some of these battles are still being fought today. I thank God that I can see the glass half full because most children or victims of abuse are unable to successfully move forward in life. Many abused children end up abusing others. Many abused children repeat the same pattern as the abuser. Often, abused children develop behavior problems leading to criminal behavior. I am grateful that God kept the commonly expected behaviors to a minimum. All praise to God for protecting my children's lives. It is because of Jesus that I can write about their successes in life. My children and I have benefited from the finished work of the cross of Jesus. As my children and I continue to fulfill the call on each of our lives, I know that by His stripes, we are healed.

Godly Parents

There are so many times that I think about my parents, and the tears begin to flow. I know that Dad died seven years ago and Mother only four years ago. Regardless of how long it has been, I can remember our times together as if they were still here. Oftentimes, when I am cooking, I think about what Mother would say to me. I can still hear Mother saying that she was glad that I was her child.

She also stated that God had blessed her to have a daughter like me, and she would not want to change me for anyone else. Mother said that I was a really good daughter. She always wanted a large family, but the Lord knew what He was doing when He gave her only one child.

When Mother was near her death, she called me one night and said, "Have you gone to bed yet?"

I answered, "No, I'm still up."

"Are you in the kitchen?"

"Believe it or not, I'm in my bedroom."

"That's good. You really need some rest. I want you to get some rest. I just called to tell you how much I love you and that truly I thank God for you. You are a wonderful daughter. You took care of me, and you took care of your dad. I don't think that any other child would have done as good a job as you did. I just want to let you know how much I appreciate you and thank you."

"You do not have to tell me thank you because if I was sick, you would have done the same thing for me."

These were the last words that Mother said to me, and I will never forget it. Sometimes, I look at the clock around 9:30 p.m. because she used to call me at 9:30 pm almost every night.

My dad stated some of the very same things that Mother said to me. He said that he and Mother both wanted more children, but God blessed them with one. The one child made up for what they had hoped for. God blessed me with many children, which are what they both wanted. Daddy also told me that they would pray over each child that I had.

Daddy was very funny at times. My children were crazy about their grandfather. He always told me that he loved me. When Daddy was near his death, he said, "I appreciate you taking good care of me while I have been sick. I am so grateful that God blessed me with such a good daughter."

I remember my grandmother telling me that she wished that I was her child. She said that I was the best grandchild that she had. My grandfather also told me the same thing. He said, "You are going to be blessed."

When I was a little girl in the fourth grade, my grandfather, said "If you ever go to college, if I'm living or dead, I am going to pay your first year of tuition." After I graduated from high school, I went to Drake Business School for about a year and a half. After I started there, my dad said,

"I did not pay the money for your tuition."

"Who paid for it?"

"Your grandfather left this money for you and told me to make sure that if you ever go to college, pay for one year for you."

My grandfather had kept his promise to me. I must admit that I am the one who was blessed with such wonderful parents and grandparents. I will never forget them. They have blessed my life in so many ways. I cherish their memories in my heart. I am grateful for their love and prayers over the lives of my children and me. I believe that my children and I have reaped the benefits of praying parents and grandparents. I thank Jesus for honoring the prayers of my parents. He deserves all the glory.

Reconnected

When my children and I left New York in 1970, we did not have the opportunity to say goodbye to any of our family members except my parents and Uncle Thomas. Our safe departure was my main priority. I prayed numerous times and listened closely for God's answer. I learned that after I pray, I must walk out my faith. For me this meant that I had to pack and prepare for departure.

Our escape from bondage went exactly according to God's plan and we arrived safely in Florida. After arriving in Florida, our communication was limited for our safety. James's sister Laura Ann wrote a letter to me. It was sent to Mother's address. I could not respond to her because I feared that James may find out about our location. The fear that was inside of me was greater than I could put into words. I feared my life and the life of my children. As a result, my children and I became separated from the Revell family without an explanation given for our abrupt departure. We were separated and hiding for more than twenty years, leaving a void and many unanswered questions to the Revell family and to my friends.

Over twenty years had passed when my son James Jr. watched a movie that provoked him to find his dad. The movie was a very emotional story about a father's fight for his sons. James Jr. began his search. Based on his own birth certificate, James Jr. saw that his dad's place of birth was Harrellsville, North Carolina, so he called the information number for that city. He looked up the name Revell, asked for information about the phone number, and called the number.

"My name is James Revell Jr. My father's name is James Revell, and my mother's name is Theodosia Revell. I don't know if I am talking to the right person, but I am trying to find out where my dad is."

"This is your Uncle Raleigh."

This was the first call that he made, and it was correct. James Jr. was excited to hear his uncle's voice on the other end of the phone. Uncle Raleigh gave James Jr. his dad's phone number and then gave him Uncle Robert's phone number. Robert was Raleigh's twin brother.

Next, James Jr. called his uncle Robert, James's brother, and spoke with him for a long time. Robert corresponded with James Jr. and sent photos of the family. Robert also gave him the phone numbers of James's sisters, Mary and Laura Ann. He called both and spoke with them as well.

James Jr. called me and all his siblings to give us contact information for the Revell family. Robert called me, and we spoke for a long time on the phone. I enjoyed talking to him. I also spoke to James's sisters Laura-Ann and Mary.

In 2004, all my children except Kenneth (because of military reasons) and Mother went to the Revell family reunion in North Carolina. Afterwards, we traveled to Wilmington Delaware to spend some time with Robert. This was a very beautiful reunion. We embraced each other, we laughed, and we cried. My children and I had the opportunity to share some of our story; we explained why we had to leave New York without communicating with any of the Revells. None of them knew why we disappeared without a trace. My children and I were emotional because of the trauma that we had endured. However, we were elated to get reconnected with the Revell family. We spent quality time embracing one of the original institutions, a family ordained by God. We realize that even though we were separated physically because of abuse, we were still connected and loved dearly by the Revell family.

Robert, a pastor and apostle residing in Wilmington, Delaware, initiated contact with our family to bring about a heartwarming reunion, with the help of James Jr. We celebrated another family reunion in August this year. We remain connected, and we support each other in special occasions and in death of family members. We look out for each other and share in celebrations. I praise God for reconnecting us to our Revell family and for the love that we have for each other. To God be the glory.

No Hospitalization

Each day I open my eyes; I realize that I have so much to be thankful for. I do not take anything for granted. I know that today was not promised to me, so I must make the best of each day that God has allowed me to see. Too often in life we become selfish and ungrateful for the many things that God blesses us with each day. In our society today, especially as a nation, we have become gluttonous and covetous to the point that we have embraced immorality to satisfy our physical desire for more.

Many people fail to appreciate the many blessings that God bestows upon them each day. I have learned to thank God for providing a roof over my head, running water, electricity, an indoor bathroom with a commode, shoes for my feet, and much more. There are so many people in this world who would call these things a luxury.

After I returned to Florida again, I valued life more than ever before. I know that if God did not protect us and deliver us from such horrendous abuse, someone or all of us would have been killed. I am very grateful that God kept us from losing our minds. The magnitude and the lengthy duration in which we suffered would have caused the average person to crack under pressure. Believe me when I tell you that there were many days we did not know if we would live to see each other the next day. I am convinced that God alone kept us safe within His hands regardless of how horrible things were.

As I reflect on the course of my life, I am happy to say that I have never been hospitalized outside of childbirth. Even more, I have never reached a point of sickness that required surgery. With all the harmful additives placed in our foods, the dangerous substances found in our water, and the contamination of the air we breathe, one would wonder how it is that we are still alive. With all the ways that the enemy has launched his attack on our bodies, I can only say that God has been more than good to me. For this, I give God all the glory.

It's All about Family

Florida was familiar territory to me because I was born in Florida, but for my children, this was a completely different culture. Even though I was born here, there were several changes that had taken place. The last time that I came to Florida to visit Mother was seven years before our abrupt departure from New York. The scenery had changed a great deal. Many of the dirt roads were now paved. There were more stores and businesses here than when I left.

On the other hand, my children had to adapt to an entirely different culture. We were so accustomed to meeting all our needs by walking only a block or two from our home. For places located much farther, we always had public transportation readily available each day. In Florida, we did not have the luxury of public transportation, and everything was located more than a few blocks away. We were challenged in communicating with other people because of our heavy New York accent and the heavy southern drawl spoken in Florida. This hampered communication between the children in school and with people in the community.

As a family, we learned to take one day at a time and make the necessary adjustments necessary to live here in Florida. We learned to accept the good things along with the bad. For instance, our living conditions were far different from the modern conveniences we shared in New York. Our house in Florida was very old and rapidly deteriorating right in front of us. We were very poor, and our income was far below the poverty line for Florida.

Oftentimes, we were embarrassed to invite someone to our home because of its poor condition and the wild kingdom (rats, roaches, lizards, and snakes) that lived with us. We did not own some of the basic luxuries such as color television, cable, air conditioning, central heat, washing machine, clothes dryer, and more. We learned to be content with what God has blessed us with, and we worked hard to achieve better living standards.

One thing that we learned early was that we always had each other. Even though we walked nearly a mile to the Laundromat with our dirty clothes in pillowcases, we did not have to *wear* dirty clothes. My children shared the responsibility of the chores around the house. When times were tight, we worked together by sharing the load. We discovered the value of connecting prayer and family as a powerful force. We faced many bumps in the road of life, and we did not always make the best choices. However, we embraced our freedom to come and go without living under tyranny.

Regardless of the struggles we faced, the joy of the Lord lived within us. As my children grew up and moved to different parts of the country, we remained very close. We took time to spend together as often as possible. When a family member is in need, we gather our resources together to meet the need. We continue to share holidays, birthdays, reunions, and special occasions together. When tragedy strikes, we stick together to lend support, and when great achievements are met, we come together in celebration.

My family has blossomed into a beautiful ray of sunshine. When we come together, the room is filled with lots of laughter and beautiful moments of joy. I love how all my children, stepchildren, daughters-in-law and sons-in-law, grandchildren, and great-grandchildren reinforce the meaning of family. Each member represents a branch of a tree that is connected to the supply source that is Christ Jesus. My family reaches beyond the bloodline and marital ties. It also includes my church family. I am grateful for many of my sisters and brothers in Christ who have stood by my side, praying and encouraging me along the way. I especially thank God for my pastor, Reverend Frederick T. Demps, for his godly leadership and consistent faith in God. I have never seen him waver from the word of God. I have seen the glory of God shine through the life of this man. I am better because of his faith and humility under fire.

I am blessed to have such loving family members who are not afraid to display the love of Christ. It's all about Jesus, and because of him, we can say it's all about family.

CHAPTER 12

Summary

God's Purpose

One of the most important questions asked by my children and me was, what was God's purpose for us in this situation? In other words, what were we to learn from this ordeal? To answer this question accurately, I had to go to the source: Jesus. This is His response in three parts.

First, the reason God allowed us to go through this horrible nightmare was to show that our family could not depend on our own strength but his. God wanted to show himself great in many ways. He wanted us to see that He'll be by our side, forever and always.

Secondly, He wanted me to be aware of the activity of demons and evil spirits. He allowed my children to have a father with a mental problem to show the power of evil influence and to show what power it can have on a person's mind. Seeing this taught us to pray and to be strong.

Lastly, God put us in this situation to show us that He loves us dearly. He wanted this family to discover His love and to build a relationship with Him. He wanted this family to be lovers of Christ. This is the reason why God chose this for us—to bring us closer to Him.

God's Timing

I have been asked this question: why did I wait so long to leave? In a conversation with my son Kevin, I took some time to try and place him in my shoes as a wife and a mother. There is more than one thing to consider when answering this question. I had to deal with a tremendous amount of ongoing fear, my duty and efforts to be a submissive wife, and my relationship with the Lord.

I had a tremendous amount of ongoing fear that was almost always present with me. Fear has a way of keeping you in place even when you want to break free. My children and I feared James because of the many ways that he dominated our lives. He treated me like a piece of property and our children as servants. My children and I feared James deeply because of the many ways he humiliated me—his constant threats to me, physical beatings to each of us, restricted freedom or lockdown mode, and his intimidation factor. James repeatedly humiliated me in front of our children.

He called me very profane names often in front of them. He frequently yelled degrading statements to make me feel like I could not live without him. James continued to tell me that if I ever thought about leaving him, no one else would want me nor want to take care of my children. James also used threats to scare me from leaving him. He made statements like, "If you ever try to leave me, I will kill you."

I was so afraid of my dad's life and the life of my children because I knew that James could carry out any of his threats. My children and I always felt like we were on lockdown. James made every effort to keep us isolated from the real world. We had a very difficult time trying to leave the house. Leaving the house sometimes equates to a sense of freedom. However, anytime that I was able to leave the house to go places such as the store or church, I was always afraid that he would be looking over my shoulder, showing up unexpectedly, or watching me from a distance.

Knowing that James frequently hid in public places often made me feel like I was being stalked. This was very scary for me. It was bad enough that I had to get permission to go anywhere. I often felt like the prison walls of bondage extended to places that I would frequent in public. The intimidation and fear were always with me. An example of this occurred one day when I went into the city to buy something. I was on the way back home, riding a subway train and sitting next to a police officer. For my safety, the police officer escorted me back to the stairway entrance to catch my next subway train. While the officer was talking to me, this overwhelming fear came over me that James was looking over my shoulder watching me. I did not feel safe. I said to myself, *I wish this man would go ahead and do his job and not follow me.* I knew that if James was watching me, there would be big trouble, and I would be accused of seeing the police officer.

When leaving the house, James always expected me to return home based on his timetable. When I returned home late from the A&P grocery store holdup James could only see me in violation of his rules. James and I lived in the same house, but we were so far apart mentally. I did not want any part of James' fantasy world of abuse and control. James did not want us to get too close to anyone. When our friends came over to visit, James's behavior would turn in an instant without warning. I also noticed that James did not want me to work outside of the home, which would have helped us financially. James also stopped the children and me from going on the field trips to nearby places. For some reason, James viewed this as a threat to him. It was clear that he wanted us to remain in lockdown and not ask any questions.

James also used intimidation tactics to try to keep me in check. Nearly every time that I was at the door talking to someone, James would stand behind the door and listen to my conversation. The person outside would not know that he was standing behind me. If I said something that James did not understand, he would come from behind the door and stare at the person with an evil eye.

James's behavior was very intimidating and embarrassing. He would physically destroy property, by punching holes in the walls, breaking furniture, and by throwing things at us. He would never take the blame for his actions but rather take his anger out on us.

The second issue that made it difficult to leave James was that I took my wedding vows very seriously. Initially, our marriage appeared very good and on the right track. I worked hard to be a good wife. I cooked, took care of the house, and was happy to work to share in the financial burden.

When the abuse started, I was ashamed, hurt both physically and emotionally, and confused as to why this was taking place. I did not understand why James had turned on me and was treating me like a piece of trash. I was confused and did not know what to do. I did not want my marriage to end in divorce like my parents' marriage. Emotionally, I was very scared to tell someone, especially my parents, because I feared that James would not only beat me but also hurt my dad. James's physical strength was far greater than the average man. I was trapped by the stronghold of fear and James's erratic violent behavior. Where would I go that James would not come after me to carry out his threats to kill me if I ever left him? I worked hard to submit to my husband the way that God designed marriage, but James made submission difficult.

The third issue that made it difficult for me to leave was because my relationship with God was not where it should have been. I knew who God was, and I knew of him through my parents, but early on, I did not have a strong personal relationship with God. My faith in God was not very strong. I was so entangled in fear that I couldn't see or hear God during our bondage. I found myself way too often looking at what I could see with my naked eyes, but I failed to see the hand of the Lord at work in my life.

There were times that I prayed to God for some things that we needed, and God answered each one of my prayers. For example, shortly after Adam was born, we ran out of food, and Thanksgiving Day was approaching. I prayed to the Lord, asking Him to provide us with food for Thanksgiving. God answered by using my dad and mom, who bought us plenty of food. We had a good Thanksgiving meal that day. On another occasion, I prayed for clothes for the children because they had outgrown their old clothes. Again, God answered by using other people who bought us new clothes and some who blessed us with money. Once, Christmas was approaching, and we did not have any money to buy gifts for the children. I remember praying to God, asking for help, and He answered me again. This time, there was a knock on our door. One of the deacons from our church came bearing gifts for all the children and for James and me. I was so grateful for the blessing.

There was yet another time in which I needed clothes for myself. I knew that I could wear my mother's clothes, so I asked her if she could help me; I assumed that she would send me some of her clothes. Instead, Mother went to the store and bought me five new dresses and bought new clothes for all the children. I remember a time in which I asked God for peace in our home and for our home to feel like a normal home. As a result, God blessed our home with peace for two to three months.

At times when things appeared calm, James would behave in a decent manner, which made me think things were changing. In the back of my mind, I would tell myself to give it a little more time and he could change. But each time that I thought I saw a glimmer of hope, James would revert to his old ways.

There were several times that I prayed for God to help us, and I thought that my prayers were not reaching heaven, the doors were shut, and I was not getting through. The worse things turned in my marriage, the more I began to think that God was not answering me. I continued to pray to God, but I failed to see His hand at work. With my naked eyes, I did not see any improvement in my marriage. I could only see a downward spiral. I did not see my marriage turning around. Things kept getting worse. The temporary periods that looked like things were getting better were only false hopes. James used these short phrases to set me up for more abuse. James's abusive behavior was repeated patterns of abuse that I failed to recognize.

It was a couple of months before our departure when I started to think differently. I realized that I had failed to see that it was God who answered my prayers for food, clothes, Christmas gifts, and some things in which I saw the physical manifestation. Then I realized that if God was answering these prayers, then I was getting through to heaven. Why would God answer these prayers and not answer my prayers concerning the abuse to my children and me?

God also showed me that I was not making the effort to get to know Christ. I wasn't reading my Bible and making time for daily devotional. God's word clearly states in Matthew 7:6–8 "Ask, and it shall be given you; seek, and ye shall find; knock, and it shall be opened unto you: For every one that asketh receiveth; and he that seeketh findeth; and to him that knocketh it shall be opened." If I wanted to find God, I needed to seek Him. God reveals Himself several ways. If I search the Scriptures, I am sure to find Him.

I also began looking back on when I was sick and the doctors told me that I had fibroid tumors and would not be able to have any more children. I remember how I prayed and fasted, and God performed a miracle that confounded the doctors. The doctors said to me, "We know that we saw something there. There are no tumors here anymore." Since then, I have had six more children. Thinking about this made me start fasting and praying again. I then started to believe and trust God that He would work things out for us.

One day, a few weeks before our departure from New York, I realized that everything was getting worse. God was in our midst all the time, but I could not see this at that time. Later in life, as I looked back in retrospect, I could see the hand of God was at work. He loved me and never left me. I also came to the realization that God was at work when things were getting worse. God allowed things to get so bad that I developed a strong desire to know Him and to leave James and not go back.

Sometimes God speaks to us, and we do not hear Him because we are inundated with our own circumstances, and the word of God cannot penetrate our lives. If we allow God to teach us how to discern and hear His voice, we can then get our joy back, and God will move in our behalf. I did not hear God's voice because the enemy's voice was speaking keep me near. The enemy kept telling me that God does not hear me and I am stuck in this madness. I was not studying His word and spending quality time with Him.

I have since learned that the more time that I spend with God, the more I can clearly hear His voice. To drown out the enemy's voice, God spoke to me in a still small voice. I listened and obeyed His instructions that this was not for me, and it was time for me to leave. This was difficult for me to understand while I was still in New York. After we arrived in Florida, God revealed to me that my delivery was ultimately in his timing. I believe that if I left earlier, I may have gone back. Earlier in my marriage, my heart was devastated, my faith was weak, and my relationship with the Lord was not strong enough for me to recognize His voice. In the last couple of weeks before our departure, I clearly heard God's voice and was willing to follow and obey Him in all things. I had come to understand that I could not leave until I was able to hear God's voice. This was important because God's will and plan for my life was the only plan that would have worked for my good.

God's Deliverance

Our situation was so bad that no one could have designed a plan of escape effectively as God did. If I followed my own of leaving, it would have failed miserably. I thought about moving in with someone close by such as Ms. Reynolds. This would not have worked because she lived too close. Trying to hide seven children would have been a huge challenge, knowing that James would have stopped at nothing until he found us. I could not go to my parents' house because that would have been the first place that he would have looked.

We needed to be relocated to a place far away from James. The plan of escape had to be perfectly designed because if any part of the plan faltered, the result could have been fatal. Our deliverance required more than just physical relocation but also protection from any future capture or enemy attacks. Once delivered, we needed supernatural protection that would keep the enemy at bay. Only God was able to deliver us and keep us safe from the enemy. I thank Jesus for loving us so much and for His deliverance and continued blessings over our lives.

God's Glory!

Everything was designed to ultimately give God the glory. Before God created me, He knew me. He knew all my issues, and he created me anyway. It was no surprise to God that my marriage would fail. He knew that James would fail in his role as a leader and protector of his family. However, I strongly believe that God anointed me with purpose that laid dormant inside of me until the time of maturity had occurred. In the meantime, He was a provider, a protector, a healer, a miracle worker, and a deliverer.

God as a Provider

In every situation in which we were backed against the wall, God provided our needs and more. There was never a time that we were left without a roof over our heads, without food to eat, and all our basic needs met. God continued to provide for us regardless of how many times we were put out by the landlords because of the destruction of property by James.

God as a Protector

Amid suffering some of the worst physical and emotional abuse, God still protected us from the worst possible outcomes. There were a few times that we should have been killed, but God did not allow the enemy to rewrite what He scripted for our lives. On numerous occasions, James's violent rage came within inches of taking our lives, but God always intervened on our behalf. In each incident, I was overwhelmed with fear. I did not always know what to do or how to respond when James's anger escalated beyond his boiling point. My maternal instincts were always to protect my children, even if it meant I had to become a human shield over them.

As I reflect over how God protected us, I realize how His timing was always perfect. On a couple of occasions, James showed up unexpectedly after I left the hair salon. As he raised his hand to hit me, a lady from the hair salon rushed over and threatened to call the police. Immediately, James departed, angry and embarrassed. During another one of James's violent episodes, he was beating me and destroying the apartment. The landlord's wife heard the disturbance and ran upstairs to my rescue. She pulled him off me, and she threatened to call the police. This marked the end of our stay at that apartment, but her intervention saved our lives.

I also remember when Mother and Papa Albert came to visit us, and James raised his hand to strike me. Thank God that Papa Albert saw him and stepped in in my behalf. Papa Albert threatened James by telling him that if he sees him raise a hand to hit me, he will not hesitate to use his gun and shoot him. Papa Albert's response caused James to back off. There were several more incidents that God used people to intervene on our behalf. In each case, God's hand of protection was upon us.

I am extremely grateful that God did not allow us to give up hope even though our situation seemed hopeless at times. For a while, I thought my prayers were not penetrating the roof of our ceiling, but God was answering my prayers. He was speaking to me, trying to let me know that this was not for me, but I was not discerning His voice. In my heart, I was hoping that God would touch James's heart, but God was saying, "Trust me, I will help you." When God opened my eyes, He drew me closer to Him. I began to clearly hear His voice, and my hope was renewed.

Each day that I wake up in my right mind reminds me that God really loves me. The magnitude of our situation could easily be viewed as sitting at death's door or embracing a mental breakdown. In either case, the outlook was depressing. It would have been easy for anyone of us to kill or be killed, give up, and take our own lives, but this course of action was not written in the script of our lives. I know that no one could have survived such a horrific ordeal except by the grace of the Almighty God.

God as a Healer / Miracle Worker

When I was diagnosed with having fibroid tumors, God performed a miracle over my body. The doctor told me that I would need to have surgery, and I could not have any more children. God not only confounded the doctors by healing me of all tumors, but He also allowed me to have six more children. The doctor's report was only a setup for God to show His power.

Two of my children, James Jr. and Juliet, were born with congenital heart defects. Both had a surgical procedure to correct the problem. Both have been free of any heart problems throughout their lives. I know that my God is a healer and a miracle worker. I am a living witness, a testimony of His healing power. He deserves all of my praise and glory.

God as a Deliverer

God is faithful to His word. Matthew 7:7–8 states, "Ask, and it shall be given you; seek, and ye shall find; knock, and it shall be opened unto to you: for everyone that asketh receiveth; and he that seeketh findeth; and to him that knocketh it shall be opened." I found God to be faithful to His word. I asked Him, and He answered me. I sought after Him and found that He was always there. I am still knocking, and I continue to see God open doors for me and my children.

Only God could have orchestrated our delivery out of bondage and despair. God delivered us from one of the worst cases of abuse and demonic attacks. He is the one who set everything in motion for our departure. First, He answered my prayer request by giving me a vision of my mother's face. Second, He changed my attitude from discouraged to encouraged. Next, He made provision and set us on course to freedom. As we enjoyed riding the freedom train, God showed me a picture of His unending love. The smiles on my children's faces and the sound of laughter echoed a future full of hope. I am reminded of:

Jeremiah 29:11 (KJV) which states, "For I know the thoughts that I think toward you, saith the Lord, thoughts of peace, and not of evil, to give you an expected end." How can I not give God the glory?

Juliet Revell-Biography

Juliet Revell resides in Jacksonville, Florida. She is a former teacher, business professional, author, and a mother. Juliet has enjoyed writing from a very young age. She discovered early in her youth that she had a natural ability to transfer visual imagery into literary artwork. It wasn't until years later that she realized her natural ability was indeed a gift from God. Juliet agreed to write From Hell to Glory: A Woman Called Theodosia to fulfill a promise made to her mother Theodosia, to bring to light to the destructive nature of domestic abuse and to deliver a message of hope to everyone in an abusive relationship.

As a child born in an abusive prison in New York, Juliet and her siblings experienced physical, emotional and verbal abuse that is difficult to fully describe in words. She and her siblings grew up not understanding why their father inflicted such brutal pain on their mother Theodosia. Numerous efforts to defend and protect their mother or to challenge their father's strange rationale only ignited harsher abuse on each of them. Too often, their mother became a punching bag or an object in which their father used to released his anger.

Growing up in this household enabled Juliet to return to the past alongside her mother and present her story to the world. This venture along with research on domestic abuse has inspired Juliet to not only honor her mother by presenting her courageous story but also to bring awareness to the elephant in our midst and to declare hope to the oppressed.

From Hell to Glory-A Woman Called Theodosia is Juliet's first published book and she is currently working on her second book. She holds a Masters of Business Administration degree and a Bachelors of Science degree in Business Management. Juliet is involved in ministry at her church, Elevate Life Church in Jacksonville, Florida and is honored to be called "daughter" of the Most High God.

Theodosia Biography

Theodosia Purifoy, resided in Palatka, Florida with her husband for over 30 years. She was a wife and proud mother of eight children, four stepchildren and a plethora of grandchildren. As a domestic abuse survivor, Theodosia understood the meaning of hopelessness and despair. Her heart's desire has always been to serve the Lord with all her heart. She graciously served and loved every person God placed in her path. Theodosia was known as a prayer warrior who was not afraid to summons heaven's attention. Her motto was always to love others as Christ loves us.

Theodosia spent years sharing her story of pain and deliverance. She strongly believed that God allowed her to experience and survive a very abusive marriage so that she could share the hope of Jesus Christ to someone else in an abusive relationship. Theodosia retired from the workforce in dietary nutrition years ago however, she continued to petition heaven for guidance to fulfill the will and purpose of God on her life. On September 30, 2024, Theodosia transitioned into her eternal home in Heaven with her Lord and Savior Jesus Christ. Her life's work and love for her children, family and friends are forever etched in our hearts.

Theodosia was a survivor because Jesus was faithful to deliver her and her children from years of abuse. Her story is presented in the book From Hell to Glory: A woman called Theodosia for all to read.